A Bull in a Glass House

José Astorga

Outskirts Press, Inc.
Denver, Colorado

A Bull in a Glass House
A Former Marine's Manifesto on Surviving the Corporate Jungle and Taking Control of
Your Life

Outskirts Press
http://www.outskirtspress.com

ISBN-10: 1-4327-0387-0
ISBN-13: 978-1-4327-0387-5

Library of Congress Control Number: 2007922103

Outskirts Press and the "OP" logo are trademarks belonging to
Outskirts Press, Inc.

Printed in the United States of America

"Regard your soldiers as your children, and they will follow you into the deepest valleys; look upon them as your own beloved sons, and they will stand by you even unto death." (Sun Tzu on The Art of War –Lionel Giles Translation)

Table of Contents

Power + Temperance = Wisdom

Introduction

Twenty years with an organization is a long time. At the end of twenty years of loyally and faithfully serving, I remain empty. This manifesto is my legacy from those years in business. A severance package is generous and nice. My manifesto is the cherry on top.

I call it a manifesto because my friend jokingly christened it as such, but after I gave it some thought, I liked it. After all, a manifesto is an opinion, a view, as all our thoughts are.

There were a few times that I thought my writing was complete, but the corporate world is a never-ending story of successes, blunders, and the overall potential for ineptitude that we as humans experience when we take a one-dimensional approach to life.

Thus, with passing time, the curtain on my stage never stayed down, and each succeeding act kept getting better and better. It kept my writing alive.

One more revision to this book (see the chapter "The Self-Fulfilling Prophecy") was warranted when I learned that the plant where I worked was being closed because of reorganization. I was offered an opportunity to relocate, which I rejected.

It is important that I mention this fact because my thoughts were being penned to paper for four years before I had even a remote thought of not working for the company I served for so long.

My career has been nothing if not a rollercoaster ride. The last ten years were full of scenes from a horror and/or comedy movie, but the last two years, well, those were a rollercoaster ride through *The Twilight Zone*. In the facility where I worked, we often searched for cameras because we thought we just had to be in the *Zone*, or *Candid Camera* was on location.

I decided that people needed to know what to expect from working for management that values the dollar and personal perks more than the employees they should be serving. Conversely, I thought it equally important that employees at all levels understand the importance of relationship building, commitment, and passion.

Employment must be a reciprocal association, which experience and many conversations have shown me is a barely understood or accepted concept; however, keep in mind that if you can relate to what you are about to read, it's not the company that's at fault; it's the leadership.

A company is simply a name that embodies a concept. It is a transparent frame, whereas the leadership, the men and women in charge, are the architects who determine the strength of that frame and the quality of what is built within it. There are some great architects out there, and there are many weak ones. I've known a few of the former and many of the latter. You see, the big picture shouldn't be just about the numbers. It has to be about the people too. It is why I say "power plus temperance equals wisdom."

Companies are in the business of making money, pure and simple. If one is fortunate enough to be associated with an organization that makes money and is philanthropic to boot, hold on tight. But make no mistake. Business is all about making money; consequently, hard decisions regarding personnel are continually made, and you never know when one of those tough decisions will hit home. Don't take it personally. It is the reality for anyone who works for someone else. Enter *The Twilight Zone*, or be featured on *Candid Camera*…either way you will experience it at some point.

My manifesto is also a lesson to all working people, the message being that we all must get off our butts, take responsibility for our lives, and do something valuable with our time. Anything that ethically brings us closer to independence and some security for ourselves and loved ones is valuable. Anything!

If there is anything a reader should take away from this book, and it will be repeated, it is that we must all dig deep within ourselves and initiate change–change that will ultimately improve and enrich our lives. Charles Darwin wrote, "It is not the strongest of the species that survives nor the most intelligent, but the ones most responsive to change." Let's face it; if this statement isn't applicable in the twenty-first century, then I don't know what is.

There will be as many interpretations of these written words as there are readers. Having said that, I quote the Greek philosopher Socrates: "The painter's product stands before us as though they were alive, but if you question them, they maintain a most majestic silence. It is the same with written words. They seem to talk to you as though intelligent, but if you ask them anything about what they say, from a desire to be instructed, they go on telling you the same thing forever." (From *Plato, The Collected Dialogues;* Edited by Edith Hamilton and Huntington Cairns)

-Think From Within-

Why the Manifesto

There is a lot of published material available on management theory and employee behavior. These writings are targeted to the business audience that is in search of a better way or some additional guidance. Some writings are theory, and some writings are based on fact. All must be applied under unique circumstances; however, many of the managers and employees that I have come in contact with either never read any of these works, skipped the human relations part of their curriculum while in school, or just plain don't give a damn.

I originally had no thoughts of publishing this manifesto, but I decided I would share my story, the benefit of hindsight, so that others could learn from my Marine Corps experience and twenty years of maneuvering the corporate obstacle course while surviving many a rough spot.

Throughout this writing I have interspersed random thoughts from my days in Marine Corps boot camp and memorable quotes or statements from the corporate funhouse. I use the term "manager" to represent managers, directors, and vice presidents.

1

To this day, I look upon my Marine Corps experience as the foundation of my determination to work hard and rise not only above myself, but also above circumstances that are not always within my control.

My audience is the employee. If you are not self-employed, then you are an employee. It does not matter if you have a college education or not. It does not matter if you are an executive or not. We are equals separated only by what drives us within and how we have navigated the environment to get to a certain place in life. Our humanity is our common bond.

The Bull Enters the Glass House

I am an employee that had been deconstructed. A rock-solid work ethic, built over years of dedication, had been challenged to the breaking point–challenged but not defeated. What do I mean by "deconstructed?" Imagine a human slowly being dismantled, like a jigsaw puzzle pulled apart until all that remains are scattered remnants of the whole.

Think of a building that, as time passed, abuse and lack of maintenance wore it down, until one day the structure just collapses.

I have witnessed employees become lifeless as a result of constant corporate bureaucracy, corporate shortsightedness, and management idiocy, and I refuse(d) to be one of them, so I took control over my situation, and I adapted. That is what the Marine Corps strengthened within me: resilience, tenacity, and the ability to adapt. It's all about the foundation. Yes, I was deconstructed, but my foundation was solid, and out of the debris rose a much stronger and wiser man.

The puzzle, once fragmented, became whole again.

When I started with the organization, I was hired at the lowest possible salary level. I started at the bottom. I was young with no experience. As I learned more about the organization, business in general, and the potential for opportunity at the new company, my inner drive and desire to succeed began to surface. I had much to learn.

To put things in perspective, when I began with the company, I did not know what the letters PC (personal computer) stood for. The most I had used was a typewriter, and I was not very good with it. I had not read a book since high school, and to tell you the truth, I do not think I read a book in high school; consequently, I became a voracious consumer of industry literature and books. As the company was growing, I was learning and applying what I learned. We grew together. As a result, over the next decade, I received various promotions, eventually making it to management. It was a lot of work and sacrifice, but I was heavily involved in the business, and I felt like I was a part of something that I helped conceive. I was enjoying the challenges placed before me.

And then slowly but surely things would begin to change around me.

The Bull is Challenged ... But Never Broken

Change, I learned, is the only constant in business—change resulting from the change in me as I evolved as an adult and as an employee, change in management, change in company structure, change in product development, change in industry developments—change, change, change.

During the period of time that "change began to change" (change begets change), if I had one regret, it is that I did not pursue further formal education. There is a proverbial "glass ceiling," and it is not easy to break. I regretted not pursuing further education only because I chose to be in the business world, and the business world places a premium on higher education. I regretted it because I thought that my career was on track, and that a degree was not necessary. Surprise! In hindsight, my judgment was impaired, not about the business, but about my importance within the organization. I thought too highly of myself. This lesson was an important one for me, "get over myself." I learned that to succeed I needed the tools that the market demanded, not the tools I thought the business needed. So I learned to define and create my own success based on my reality.

We are an accumulation of our life's experiences and life's lessons. We grow into what we think or ideate; however, we as humans have a tendency to blame the world around us for everything that befalls us. People need to have heroes, have faith, and to have hope. There also seems to be a need to pass blame; "it's in his genes." Wow, even our genetics are not exempt from the blame game. It is our permission to take the easy route. A perfect example is the often-heard statement at work, "I don't get paid to do that" or "It's not my job." My friends, it is very simple...you either accept the consequences of your decisions and try to do the best that you can at whatever you do, or you take control of your environment, change your circumstances, and then do the best that you can at whatever you do. But before you can do that, you have to understand your reality.

Long ago I did the blame thing, and it got me nowhere. As I write this, I am still evolving, still learning, still making mistakes, but I never give up. I have no heroes, my faith has been sorely tested, and hope has all but evanesced. What I do have, as solid as rock, is the knowledge that I am in control of me—my reality, not my genes, not any hero, not my hope, and certainly not anyone else.

"You must never confuse faith that you will prevail in the end–which you can never afford to lose–with the discipline to confront the most brutal facts of your current reality, whatever they might be." –Admiral Jim Stockdale, former POW interviewed by Jim Collins, author of *Good to Great*

The Bull's Experience

So here I am twenty years later with many experiences and lessons learned. This writing was a few years in the making (on and off). I started it as a catharsis, a way to relieve tension, a way to deal with the lunacy that we are often engulfed in when we are dealing with the egotist, the tyrant, the disconnected, or the misguided. But here is where my perception and my reality came to a crossroad. Was it me or was it everyone around me? I was actually told once "There is no policy against bad management." Great support structure. Here is where the corporation, with its so-called Human Resource Department and funky rules and regulations fails the employee. What are the options? Speak up and get blackballed (I tried speaking up), don't speak and stew, look for another job in a lousy economy? Nah ... I found comfort within myself, and I took control. I handled things my own way, and I survived the lunacy–the corporate jungle.

A few descriptions of me as defined by my Ivory Tower leaders: "diamond in the rough," "bull in a china shop," "stubborn," "not a team player," etc. I will admit there were times I should have kept my mouth shut, and there were times that–at least early on–my inexperience got the best of me. But everything I did or said was one hundred percent from the heart and for the organization. I clearly wore my passion on my sleeve, and it hurt my prospects and garnered me a reputation as a loose cannon, "A Bull in a Glass House." As a result, I learned to control my passion and all but extinguish it, until I chose to ignite it.

> Manager to author: *"You're a blue-collar worker trying to cross over into a white-collar world."*

Do I have a problem with authority? Maybe, but I really don't think so. I definitely have a serious problem with ignorance and blatant disregard for others, disregard for justice, disregard for truth, disregard for reality, and even more so when the ones in charge exhibit this behavior. I have seen more of these types of managers than I care to remember. I often wonder what causes someone to turn into a butthead when he or she gains some authority or power.

Over the latter ten years of my career, I inherited new management, and executive management began turning over, all of which had a dramatic effect on the corporation and employee attitudes; consequently, that feeling of belonging, of ownership, that I possessed early on began to dissipate. The new managers thought they had all the answers. Why? Partly because of their experience and mostly because of their confident arrogance. The new managers also wanted new talent—new blood, degreed blood—and I was old news.

I was old news. That was probably one of the most painful realizations and lessons of my twenty years.

A national-level management position was created. Some, including me, thought it was a given that I would get the job, but management had other ideas. The upper level managers thought I was not fully qualified. I knew they were bugged by my lack of a college degree, but I believed my work ethic, my experience, and my commitment would get me through. I was wrong.

Some were surprised. I was devastated.

The man they hired for the position was a good fit for the type of management that would evolve over the next few years, one in which I was not a good fit.

Unfortunately the hurt of being bypassed for the promotion was greater than I would admit to myself or anyone else. Sometimes it manifested itself in my dealings with the new management team. But, time passed and wounds healed. There would be many more challenges and surprises to keep me distracted.

That damned degree! But I was persistent, and I did not disappear or make it easy on anyone to just set me aside. To some extent, I won management over by constantly selling myself and making myself visible, so managers began placing me on high visibility projects that turned out to be relatively successful, depending on how you define "success." These projects eventually turned out to be my own little internal market niche.

But in the end, while others received promotions for their efforts and my contributions, I was left to wade in the tides of endless bureaucracy that result as the organizational chart gets deeper and deeper. Everyone needs an empire.

That issue wouldn't bother me much, except that the deeper the organizational chart becomes, the more bureaucracy, ignorance, and narrow mindedness gain a foothold on the genetic makeup of the organization.

Apparently the deeper the organizational chart grows the thicker the wall of delusion grows between management at the top and operating employees at the bottom. A few examples follow.

A long-term employee and colleague applied for a position as a manager in his particular department. During the interview he was told that to succeed in his particular field, he needed to become more "Hollywood."

"More Hollywood?" Are you for real?!

I know some of these Hollywood types, and it basically describes a person who dresses sharp, speaks very well and quickly, is always talking, kisses serious tail, and can blow more steam up management's butt than required for a hot air balloon. Most of them, maybe not all of them, but most bring nothing of substance to the table. They can talk their way out of almost any situation. It is nauseating to watch, yet at the same time entertaining. "Hollywood(s)" are kings of the bureaucracy. It is how they survive and thrive.

My colleague did not pursue the position.

Here is another small (out of many) but amusing example of bureaucracy where a vice president from another department had a question. I know that he knew the answer would have to come from my department, and this man knew me, but he sent the question to the vice president of my department, who forwarded the question to the director or my department, who forwarded the question to the manager of my department, who forwarded the question to me. What could have taken a few minutes, took half a day. Whatever happened to picking up the phone? Email is a great tool, but it is often misused or overused.

And lastly, during a period of empire building, one of the corporate managers offered me additional responsibility at another location. Normally, I would never refuse the possibility of growth; however, there were extenuating circumstances. The main one of all was that the location I was being assigned already had a manager who did the job quite well, and I knew him. If that wasn't enough, the location was a large facility that had plenty of managers and employees in positions similar to mine who could accomplish the same job.

The additional responsibility would also require regular travel, which meant the incurrence of unnecessary expenses for no real business reason other than the extension of power. I also reasoned that some day (wishful thinking) someone would be placed in charge who questioned silly moves such as this one. I turned down the offer, much to the chagrin of the corporate manager. It just made no business sense, and it ended up being a very good decision on my part as the company evolved and management continued to turnover.

Summing It Up

The last ten years for me have been full of scenes straight out of a horror movie, at the very moment when the hallway suddenly seems endless and that door you so desperately want to reach fades farther away into an endless pathway. My frustration with the business of which I have been a part is not just about effort and reward; it is about the lack of appreciation, honesty, and loyalty. My frustration is about employees who become a number and a means to an end...never mind the method. Honesty? You have got to be kidding. Loyalty, appreciation? What's that? You often hear these words from management in one form or another, but most are condescending statements. Generally speaking, the "not invented here," the "what have you done for me lately," and the "hidden agenda" are pervasive in a company.

I can control my education and my immediate environment, but I can only attempt to influence how others generally view me and view themselves and how we all interact.

Sometimes we must reach beyond ourselves.

In twenty years, I have rarely witnessed an executive or manager reaching out to the employees, or, for that matter, employees reaching out to the leadership. We all think we are owed something, and our behavior is driven by this flawed conviction. The focus is and has been solely on the search for short-term profit, bonus points, and self-preservation. By contrast, in the Marines, the search is for discipline, team cohesiveness, and winning. "We know that it is the hits that count. We will hit."(Excerpt from Rifleman's Creed) It is a contrast of management vagaries and intimations as opposed to the brute force of having a clear vision and objective…preparedness for victory.

I am neither the first to be deconstructed nor will I be the last. Over the years, I have witnessed the mass demoralization of employees. I have learned the power of image and presentation, or how to bullshit your way through business. I have learned the true meaning of the old saying, "What have you done for me lately," when it comes to management's appreciation of an employee.

I have learned that individuals must take responsibility for their own careers and not trust that someone else will do the perceived right thing. My expectations were no one else's obligations. I have learned that the only constant is change, complacency is a death march, and loyalty is fleeting. I have learned that success is only partly dependent on the capabilities of an individual; the rest has to do with character, position, timing, and context. These experiences and knowledge prompted me to assess myself, my situation, those around me, and how others view me, and I am better and stronger for my experiences. I press on. Press on…it is what happens in life. It is required for survival and success. It is how I have made it through my most difficult times, by charging forward and through glass walls.

I have concluded that business makes us caricatures of ourselves. We exaggerate our beings and depreciate our humanity. I have witnessed over and over again the cartoonish behavior of individuals who think more of themselves than anyone else could possibly think of them–the arrogance, the vanity, from employees to executive management. It's like being on an episode of the reality show *Survivor,* the only difference being that in *Survivor* the game is out in the open and it lasts only about thirty-nine days. At the office, most people have hidden agendas, and the game lasts as long as the employment.

All the education in the world cannot teach a person how to be humble or balance her ego for the sake of solid relations and corporate success. It can be faked for a while, but the real person is eventually exposed; often, after the damage is done–lots of damage.

I am amazed when I come across an article on executive coaching. There is a whole industry out there of people who master the art of turning senseless assholes into sensing beings. Thankfully, there are many successful, humble executives. They are not afraid to show their human side and are still very effective. But if a company board has to hire a coach to help an executive get in touch with his human side, then the corporation has failed. Think about it. When you get to this level in a career, you supposedly have demonstrated the skills of a successful leader. If it becomes apparent that the individual does not have "what it takes," he needs to go, just like it happens at lower levels. I can only surmise that coaches are used because placing a narcissist or schizophrenic in charge would reflect badly on the stock price, or the company has invested too much in the executive to just "throw him away." I say go for it. Acknowledge the mistake and move on. By the time this person is coached, the damage is already done to employee morale and or client relationships.

There is nothing wrong with an executive receiving training or coaching to improve a skill or a weakness. We all need continued improvement. Also, anyone who experiences a sudden condition that results in a personality swing deserves patience and understanding. But a personality trait is ingrained and cannot be wished away. Self-change requires personal reflection and it takes conviction for someone to take the initiative and follow through. I know...I have been there, and I had no coach. Self-transformation requires a level of introspection not necessarily innate to humans.

During my career, I have reported to many different managers with many different personalities. In fact, I would say some of the managers had many personalities.

My schooling has been the corporate web of possibilities. My classroom has been the job, and my teachers have been my experiences and those with whom I come in contact. I have talked with many employees about their own unique situation, and I have given as well as received advice, all the while learning and evolving.

"Get rid of self conceit. For it is impossible for anyone to begin to learn that which he thinks he already knows." (Greek philosopher Epictetus)

15

For the purpose of this writing, I view the past twenty years as on-the-job research of myself, corporate behavior, and the employee perception of corporate life.

As I write this I am aware of the powerful influence and struggle between perception and reality. We humans are often mired in our own thoughts and needs without regard for the simple fact that we are not alone. We are a part of something bigger. Compare politics to business. How is it that politicians, so educated and supposedly committed to their constituencies, can be so diametrically opposed to solutions that will benefit the public that they serve? There are as many answers as individual thought could possibly conceive. What is right? In whose eyes? As a result, I have to choose what I learn, what I believe, and, most importantly, I choose my reality.

The Bull's Survival Guide

In a nutshell, corporate survival is about competence and relationships, just like in the Marines. If I were to come up with a very short recipe for survival or success it would have to be: Competence, Passion, Relationships (CPR). My experience has taught me all three—not just one or another—are required in varying degrees.

Competence can be defined as the ability to effectively complete one's job requirements. As an operations manager, I have learned that there are basically three levels of competence.

Practical competence is the ability of someone to complete basic tasks. There is minimal creativity required. If an employee is trained and can effectively follow basic processes and procedures, then the employee can be considered competent.

Adaptive competence is the next level up from practical. At this level of competence, an employee has the ability to take fundamental business processes and procedures and adapt them to varying conditions. This employee is inherently more effective because if there is anything we know about business, it is that nothing stays the same. Adaptive competence enables an employee to modify his or her behavior to changing conditions.

Finally there is expert competence. The employee that has become an expert at his position is at the peak of his game. This individual not only knows the job inside and out, he also grasps the bigger picture and can function effectively with other departments. He is able to make decisions in a nonlinear fashion and requires minimal or no immediate supervision.

There are varying degrees of competence within the three levels identified. For example, an employee could border between adaptive and expert. But competence is not the end all be all . . . if you want the "right employee."

Competence can be taught; however, I have known many competent people who are either philosophically ignorant or productively lazy.

By philosophically ignorant (P.I.) I mean employees who lack introspective abilities. They have a minimalist approach to empathic management, and their moral imperative is making a name for themselves at almost any cost.

The productively lazy (P.L.) employee may or may not be P.I. oriented, but he is a master of job definition. The job description is his personal roadmap, the compass points only south, and all roads are one-way. His mantra is typically "I don't get paid to do that."

On the other hand, emotions such as passion, caring, integrity, or empathy cannot be taught only nurtured. Let me be clear: I am a strong believer and proponent of relationship building. Be nice. But I am also a strong believer that there are times not to be nice. It is a never-ending balancing act of introspection, self-control, and circumstance.

What follows is my humble attempt at leading, sharing knowledge and experience, and, as much as possible, bridging the gap between management and the employee and between the employee (including management) and perception.

This list of observations and principles gleaned from twenty-three years of experience are not all-encompassing; there are hundreds of "how to" books. I certainly did not invent them. There is no rule on how to apply them. I do not profess to have all the answers, and I am sure there are people out there who would accuse me of being guilty of some of the very things I am talking about. And without question, I have made mistakes.

I have lived through periods of unconscious existence where I allowed environment to dictate my reality; however, in all cases, I ultimately dug deep, took control and grew as a result of my experiences.

I value these principles, and I hold myself accountable . . . always.

> *"The height of injustice is to seem just without being so."* (Plato, *The Collected Dialogues*)

19

The Bull's Rules

Communication

1) Communicate openly, honestly, constantly. Communication is a two-way street that must be voluntarily walked. It is up to management to create the atmosphere that promotes this kind of interaction. Lack of communication is probably one of the biggest reasons for the demise of many personal and professional relationships. Communication- encourage it. Practice it.

"You're making my ears bleed."
–Author to coworker who could not get to the point

Tact is a critical element of communication. What you say is important, but how you say it is just as or more important. Tact and judgment often set the stage for success or failure in any exchange. A person's reaction to any statement can be swayed by how the statement is delivered, e.g., timing, body language, vocal pitch, or eye contact.

Manager: *"I can't believe you said that."*
Author: *"But it's the truth."*

Author: *"Maybe I could have used more tact."*

Manager to author: *"Keep your communication clear and precise."*

In the Marines, communication is a prerequisite for success. In boot camp, communication is crisp and to the point—no ambiguity. I never saw battle, but the consequence of anything less than crisp communication is clear.

Extreme communication: I have often been in meetings, presentations, or just one-on-one communication where individuals cannot seem to put aside their portable communications device, regardless of what it is, e. g. cell phones. It is very rude to interrupt people for no apparent reason than your perception of your importance in this world. There is no universal rule that the evolution of technology must breed ignorance of common courtesy. Don't be rude.

Patience and Group Communications

2) When communicating, make an effort to understand the intended audience. Different personalities require different approaches. Not everyone processes information the same way and at the same time. Not everyone learns in the same fashion. Not everyone communicates in the same manner.

I used to think I had a learning disability. I had a difficult time with certain things. Heck, it takes me months to memorize my own phone number. But I learned. I learned that the problem wasn't necessarily always me; it was the fact that I was expected to learn like everyone else and at the same pace as everyone else, and it just doesn't work that way.

Patience and understanding will allow productive communication. Adapt to differences in communication styles. This is certainly not easy for everyone. I actually have to work at this since I am not the most patient person. To add to my predicament, I have a slight speech impediment. I have issues with the letters *R* and *L* that I am very aware of, and sometimes this awareness makes it worse. Talking to me can be like talking to Elmer Fudd on a caffeine overdose. But the results of working on communication are certainly worth the effort in the form of clarity, understanding, acceptance, and results.

> Author: *"I'll have a Yuengling."*
> Bartender: *"Sorry?"*
> Author: *"A Yuengling!"*
> Bartender: *"A what?"*
> Author: *"Give me a Budweiser."*

During an exchange, when one or more individuals exhibit a limited ability to understand or accept the bigger picture or reality of a situation, an objective person is needed to mediate the communication. Unfortunately in business, the employee rarely, if ever, has this luxury.

> Manager to author: *"I can't make you understand. I can only help you to understand."*
> (Note: One of us did not succeed)

Meetings are a great form of communicating business requirements, but meetings are often a waste of time. When scheduling and conducting meetings, managers must ensure that the time is appropriate and that focus is maintained on the reason for the meeting. In other words, address the issues and get out. Some feel that because they have time on their hands, everyone else does. Bad assumption.

> Author: *"Can we take a break for lunch? I need to eat."*
> Manager: *"We are in the middle of a very important meeting."*
> Author: *"I can't think straight I'm so hungry. I have to go."*
> (Note: the meeting was concluded after lunch, apparently many of the attendees were also hungry, but no one else spoke up.)

Smoking in groups is not a meeting, it is not tax deductible, and it is not productive. Why do organizations, even under constant pressure to improve efficiency, continually permit the "perpetual smoke break?" I've seen employees spend more time on smoke breaks than they do on lunch. Add those hours up for a year. What is it that makes it acceptable for a person that smokes to waste so much time throughout the day? I like to drink beer. Maybe I will take beer breaks throughout the day.

Smoking is a personal habit that adds absolutely no value. Do it on your own time. If you have a medical condition that requires you to smoke during the day in excess of your assigned breaks, by all means bring in a doctor's note.

Listening & Discipline

3) Listen objectively and intently–not an easy thing to do. We are bombarded daily with a ton of information from many

sources, but often we are distracted or interpret the messages incorrectly, mostly as a result of selfishness or impatience.

A manager told me that people's impressions of him were their own perceptions and problems and not his concern. What this man failed to see was that he was so hung up on himself and his own abilities that he just did not care what anyone thought. Public perception was not necessarily wrong. This manager just did not know how to process information that was not in line with how he viewed himself and his environment. A good rule of thumb is that if enough people claim something, their claim warrants investigation.

Manager to author: "*I don't care what you think.*"
Author: "*What a surprise.*"

Coworker to author: "*Here comes the crocodile.*"
Author: "*Why do you call him that?*"
Coworker: "*All mouth, no ears.*"

I have worked with many people who just do not know how to listen. The most common example is when I am telling a story or answering a question. I apparently say something that triggers a memory response in the person I am speaking to. This person then interrupts the flow of conversation to share his or her own experiences or recollected knowledge. Sometimes I let it go. Sometimes I say something like, "Stop. Please let me finish." Sometimes I am not so polite.

Manager to author: *"You take me on a train ride, but never drop me off where I need to be."*
(Note: I have a very short attention span, this individual had none. It is one of my favorite and funnier quotes, especially since I'm not really sure what he meant. But you had to be there. We still joke about it today.)

In the Marines, listening and following instructions are prerequisites for survival. Listening is a discipline. Discipline is a foundation that pervades everything a Marine does and is inherent in every principle presented here. Success requires discipline. Survival mandates it.

I'd like to share a personal example of discipline. My father was an excruciatingly heavy smoker. He was a strong man, but like many of us, he was bound by his past, and it would doom his future.

After a scare and a visit to the hospital, a doctor told Dad, "Stop smoking or die." He stopped smoking. My dad never picked up another cigarette. It wasn't easy, but he did it. Dad later died of varying complications.

No excuses, no whining . . . nothing–he just quit and never looked back. One might argue that he had no choice, but he made a choice, even though it may have been too late. This one act showed me that some "diseases" or "addictions" are decisions. It takes discipline and strength to give up a dependency, and it is also a decision–a decision to be disciplined.

In The Trenches

4)   In order to get a true reading on the pulse of morale and

25

opinion, management must make the time to talk to front-line employees with no fear of retribution. Although talking to everyone may not be possible or practical, if a manager talks to enough people he or she will get a true read on employee attitudes. Often executives rely on their immediate subordinates for information, but these executives do not realize that they are receiving skewed and biased data. Get in the trenches; make the time. Make it a priority.

Leaders must never, ever accept one side of a story. Employees are often misquoted or events are often strongly embellished so that someone can achieve a desired result.

A manager I know once quoted me as having said something I never said. This individual had a feeling he wanted to express to executives and believed that by saying he was quoting me, more weight would be added to his particular emotion. When I found out about it, I just shook my head. The situation wasn't important enough to me to warrant my time. Sometimes you just have to go with your instincts.

Management may achieve good or great statistical results, but at what expense of ethics or employee morale? Executives must know and understand what is happening at all levels and why. I can't stress enough how important it is for leaders to get in the trenches and keep their fingers on the pulse of their operation.

Often I feel like I am working in two organizations. On one hand you have the rah-rah group at the top with their questionable measurements and wonderful stories of success and camaraderie. Then you have everyone else, the people who actually accomplish something, who read or hear about these stories and can only wonder, "What company are they referring to?" Organizations need convergence between realistic expectations that flow from the top and actual results at the operational level, and convergence will be achieved only by cutting through the crap. How do you cut through the crap? Start by eliminating the dead wood and the "Hollywoods."

"You really need to get out there and talk to everyone. Can't you see what is happening?"
Author to manager

Coworker to author about corporate: *"They really are a bunch of geniuses out there!"*

During one of my long-term assignments, things reached a boiling point between my manager and me. Communication between us had become limited, forced, and I sensed that I was on a short bridge. He viewed me as a major thorn in his side, and I . . . well, I don't know. He was trying to change me, I was trying to change him, and the only change was growing anger and resentment. No one would listen. No one!

I was working in a room (project war-room) full of people when I received an e-mail from my boss. Without any notice, communication, or even hint to me, he distributed an announcement that my area of responsibility had been stripped from me. Of course, this was done for my own good because I was so immersed in the project that I was working on. I immediately knew that I was being set up, and another colleague was been dragged onto the field of battle. It was a battle that, in the end, would have no victors.

As I read the announcement, I could feel my anger rising within me. The next thing I remember, my laptop computer was streaking across the table with my fist firmly imprinted on a now shattered computer screen. The screen looked like a lightning storm over the horizon.

The room grew completely silent. No one said a word. One of my closest friends was sitting right across from me. I can describe the look on her face only as a combination of horror and shock and maybe even a little fear. I was extremely frustrated and angry. My anger had been building for months. I have since learned to channel that energy, and you are reading one of those channels.

My friend stood, rushed around the table, and walked me outside where she helped me regain my balance and composure. Thank you for being there.

What about my laptop?

I had a very good relationship with our Information Technology Department. I approached someone in that department and explained, on the record, that I had dropped my laptop. Off the record, I disclosed what happened. The person knew my manager, understood the circumstances, and repaired my laptop. Thank you for understanding.

> Author to manager: *"If you allow this man to continue on this ridiculous path, I will not forget it."*

Hierarchy

5) The more hierarchy in an organization, the more removed management is from reality. By the time information reaches the top, it will have been filtered more times than bottled water. I have learned that a well-trained and motivated group of individuals does not require multiple levels of management. Reduced levels of management permits speed in the operations. Speed is a prerequisite for success in today's world.

During one particular project, I told the executive in charge to let me handle the particulars simply because my department had the skills to complete the mission efficiently. The scope of the project was such that the more people were involved, the more opportunity for mistakes existed. I explained the situation to him, but he insisted that every function had a department, and that department needed to handle its particular function. Consequently, what could have been handled by one or two individuals in one location ended up being handled by four or five individuals spread out across the country, and of course, the problems increased in scale.

It was, and remains, as clear as a beautiful sunny day to me that if there were fewer meetings, fewer conference calls, less talking, more flexibility, and much more doing, things would have been done!

Author to colleague: *"Was anything accomplished on that call?"*
Colleague: *"Absolutely nothing."*

"Does anyone do any work in that facility? All chiefs, no Indians."
Coworker to author on stream of promotional announcements

Empathy

6) Show empathy for each other, bottom-up and top-down. A leader must be able to put himself in the shoes of employees at any level. If the needs of employees are not considered and sufficiently met, organizational objectives will not be reached.

"Go home and take care of your wife. Don't worry about anything else."
Author to coworker

I have witnessed the verbal thrashing of employees who did not speak quickly enough or act in a fashion consistent with what a manager believed he should be hearing or seeing. The manager refused to accept individual thought processes and communication styles. Eventually employees adapt attitudes of speaking only when they have to. The relationship becomes forced without any empathy on the part of management.

One night in bed, while in boot camp, I had to pee real badly … BAD. Keep in mind that once in bed, you are not permitted to get out. I was not about to wet myself, so I sneaked into the head (bathroom). As I finished and was about to leave, I ran smack into the drill instructor. He was just standing there with his arms folded, a pit-bull stare on his face. I braced myself for the worst.

He asked me what I was doing, and I responded, "S*ir, the private will take anything the drill instructor can dish out, before the private pees on himself.*" (We were not allowed to use the word "I"). The drill instructor stepped aside and I, remarkably, was spared his wrath. In retrospect, I suspect the drill instructor placed himself in my shoes.

Team Work & Fighting Complacency

7) Promote teamwork and appreciate individualism. A cohesive team is composed of individuals. By recognizing the unique elements of individual behavior and how it can benefit a team, team members can function as a unit without losing their identities.

A team cares about each other's individual success and the overall team success. A team should not be just a group of individuals who meet deliverables. A strong team will insist on quality not only in their work, but also in their relations. Not everyone on a team will always like each other, but individuals must respect everyone else on the team. It takes effort. It takes commitment. It takes leadership.

A manager cannot know everything. No one knows it all. The sooner you learn this fact in life, the better. Acknowledge this simple fact and surround yourself with a good, strong team. When building a team, strengthen your weaknesses and challenge your strengths.

It is helpful to have a confidant, one person you know will stick with you through thick and thin and will always tell you the facts. This kind of relationship develops. It cannot be fabricated. Having a confidant has helped me to cope with many of the crazy situations I have found myself in. It is good to surround yourself with individuals who keep you grounded.

Coworker to author: *"You need to play their game."*
Author: *"I'm having a very difficult time with this particular game, but I will try."*
Coworker: *"Try harder!"*

Manager to author: *"I don't want you helping anyone. I want you internally smart, externally stupid."*

The Marines are a team, pure and simple. No room for egos. In boot camp, be a team player, or do not close your eyes at night.

In looking back, I can remember only once when I was a weak link in a team. I just did not belong, and neither did I agree with much of what these individuals said or did, and I was vocal about it—and it got me in trouble. It was the most difficult time of my career, and only circumstances and leveraged opportunity changed the outcome to my favor. In this particular scenario, the individuals were much more valuable than the team.

Author to coworker: *"This isn't a team, it's a cult."*

During this time, the irony of it all was that I provided emotional support and functioned as a sounding board for some of the other team members who were having difficulty gelling with the expectations of the team.

I recognized that I was a disruptive influence, but what my mind told me I should be doing—if anything, just to

32

keep the peace–my spirit was rebelling, in a big way. I knew what I needed to do to fit in, but I could not bring myself to do it. The Bull in me simply could not be tamed.

When it came to running the department, the team leader and I did not always see eye to eye. It was his approach that made me steam. The twist here is that outside of work, we had developed a strong bond. The deterioration of the relationship between this individual and me was one of my all-time disappointments. Had I quit, we probably would have remained good friends.

Why didn't I quit? To me it wasn't an option. Why wasn't it an option? Was it lack of preparedness, fear of the unknown, complacency? I know the answer. It can be any one of those reasons, and it will not happen again.

We get jobs, we develop habits, and we become dependent on those habits. It is a dependency almost as bad as an addiction, yet we do not realize it until the time arrives–and it always does–that we have to make a choice. The problem is that for most of us there are no choices, because our complacency has prevented us from preparing for the unknown. How do we prepare for the unknown? We "unlazify", take control of our lives and emotions, and expand our horizons. We must break our self-imposed bonds. We must give up the dependency on complacency.

"I can't ignore the writing on the wall. I have to exert whatever influence I can on the organization . . . for my people. I am trying to lead. I have been following long enough. This one time . . . just this one time . . . I need to lead."

Author to management on changing events and controlling outcomes

Performance

8) Non-performers must be eliminated. Employees who consistently do not meet objectives or who have bad attitudes will hurt the business, and their attitude will slowly spread. Employees performing at lower than average levels must elevate their performance or be eliminated. The best measure of performance is the result; however, it is imperative that results be achieved ethically and equitably.

In boot camp non-performers were handled decisively. The recruits took care of this issue themselves, if they had to, or the non-performers disappeared into an extended tour until their performance improved. The extreme cases were released. The good thing about the manner in which non-performers were handled was that Marines in training did not suffer from the need for political correctness.

> Author: *"I have to let you go. I have tried everything, and you just can't get here when we need you."*
> Employee: *"It's not you, it's me. I understand."*

Motivation

9) Motivation is intrinsic. It is a personal attribute. Not everyone is motivated in the same fashion; however, there is one constant. The lower the employee wage, the more weight the employee places on money. It is important to understand what motivates employees.

Employee: "*I need a raise.*"
Author: "*So do I.*"

I believe that motivational needs should morph as a person climbs the corporate ladder. At the lower end of the pay spectrum we need to meet our unique needs and seek to be personally gratified. As employees reach new levels of responsibility and compensation, the need for self-gratification should diminish, and motivation is drawn outwards. Helping others succeed should motivate at this level. This is where leaders need to lead and practice some of these principles. I never did understand managers, directors, or vice presidents jockeying for credit against those who served them best. Hey, dummy, you have achieved something. Let someone else shine.

In the Marines we motivated each other through competitions. Often just completing some of the challenges placed before us was motivation enough. In boot camp, the goal of proudly wearing the Eagle, Globe, and Anchor was motivation. Companies can motivate their employees simply by treating them honestly and fairly and actually putting into practice their mission and values.

Throughout my career, I was not allowed much latitude in the giving of incentives to employees, so I had to get creative. When it comes to motivation, I had two types of employees, and I'll explain by example.

One type of employee understood the unfortunate pay limitations of a position; regardless, no matter what those employees did, they gave it their all. They were simply underpaid when measured against effort and result. For these individuals, overtime was never a question. If I

35

needed them Saturday or Sunday, they were available, and they did whatever they had to, whenever they had to. For these employees, I would walk through walls.

Had policy allowed it, I would have eliminated one position and taken some percentage of that salary and split it between two or three of these individuals. Fewer employees, more money, more productivity–an all-around win.

Then I had the other type of employee, the deserving ones. These employees watched the clock and made sure they earned every cent for every hour they worked. They did only what they were told, had barely any initiative, and if a shortcut was available, right or wrong, they would find it. These employees were often average and on occasion good employees, but they limited themselves because of the "me" focus. They were given what they earned–no more, no less. There was nothing really wrong with those employees' behavior when they produced, but there was no comparison with the employee who had fire and desire.

See Appendix A for more on motivation and self-improvement.

Unselfishness

10) Don't take credit for the team's accomplishments; always take responsibility for the team's failures. How often have we all heard that one? Many preach it–few practice it. I have known managers who must share in all of their team's accomplishments in some form or fashion. Do not take the moment away from employees.

36

Author to coworker: "*I want you to shine.*"

I have known managers who took credit for most of what their employees did. No matter what an employee did, some of these guys made sure everyone knew that management influenced the outcome.

I often wonder how some employees manage through the minutia of life without being instructed by their manager every step of the way–if I were to only listen to the manager.

"*Mind your own business.*"
Manager to author after pointing out to manager his credit taking

Strong leaders are not selfish. Strong leaders place the needs of their followers and their organization above all else. In a positive environment, professional growth and recognition should follow in line with results.

Unselfishness should not be a means to an end; it transcends conscious motive. If you help others and always expect something in return, it is not unselfishness, it is manipulation.

Appreciation

11) A leader thanks his employees. Sometimes a heartfelt thanks and pat on the back will motivate or lift up a sagging spirit, at least in the short term. Show some appreciation. Personally, real appreciation motivates me, and it doesn't cost a dime.

"I am you. Thank you for all that you do."
From author's talk to department

There are many ways to show employees appreciation. One easy method, for those in operations, is to allow the vendors to bring in pizzas or pass along sporting tickets when they are made available. From what I have seen, it is an industry standard that promotes improved communications and places increased visibility on the vendor's company. This giving provides an opportunity for managers to transfer these gifts to employees as one more form of appreciation. I am talking about things like tickets, dinners, T-shirts, etc. The most important thing is that no reciprocity must be involved.

Prior to management changes, we would do things like allow an occasional extended lunch or organize a small barbeque where everyone contributed something. During Thanksgiving we would organize a Thanksgiving luncheon. One year, I purchased a whole pig and had it cooked. It was a great way to bring everyone together, and it didn't cost the company anything, other than some time to show employees they are valued.

Praise

12) Give praise only when deserved. Anything else is boring, grandstanding rhetoric not worth transmitting. Don't make every little incident an Academy Award presentation.

Some people are so enamored of their own spoken word that they insist on turning every opportunity, no matter how small, into a lavish oral presentation. Individuals dread having conversations with them. On the faces of audience members, I have witnessed the expressions of disbelief at the level that some presenters will go to, and yet those presenters do not have a clue about audience reaction or they just don't care. Either way, the result is the same: people tune them out.

Colleague to author after attending long, long meeting: *"I have never met anyone so in love with the sound of his own voice."*

Integrity

13) Beware of the employee who practices situational ethics- at some point, it will be practiced on you. Never ask an employee or vendor to compromise integrity. I once sat in a meeting in which a manager demanded proprietary information from a partner vendor, but for the vendor to answer would have compromised his ethics. I was embarrassed for the manager, for the vendor, and for myself for having to listen to it. After the meeting, I approached the manager regarding his behavior, and he had not realized what he had done. Perhaps he was caught up in the moment.

"I'm not perfect."
Manager to author

We must always be aware of the immutable fact that thought precedes all action.

Companies and individuals can attempt to define ethics on paper, and a written definition is required as a form of guidance, a template for doing what is right because we are human and humans need guidance. But like some laws, written ethics can be prejudiced based on the experience of the authors. I believe true ethics are an extension of our natural (no one is born bad) human propensity to further the good, whatever the good may be. Anything other than that violates what some call the natural law. It seems rather simple to me. Those who do harm violate the natural law, and those who do not do harm perpetuate the natural law. Natural law is the view that human nature or the universe governs morality. This concept is very deep stuff, but *naturally* makes sense to me.

One definition of integrity in *Webster's Dictionary* is the quality or state of being of sound moral principle; uprightness, honesty, sincerity. Sacrifice integrity, and you weaken your core self, which can lead to self destruction.

Human beings are no angels, and I do not claim to be one, but a Marine's integrity and his honor are his bond.

One year I was told I needed to promote three team leaders.

> Author to manager: *"What the hell is a team leader?"*
> Manager: *"A supervisor."*
> Author: *"Why don't we just call them supervisors?"*
> (Note: Human resources loved this concept because it simplified job descriptions.)

At first I resisted promoting three supervisors because I didn't need those positions. But, I was told that I wasn't seeing the bigger picture, even though that didn't change the fact that I didn't need three supervisors. The only positive thing that came out of this situation was that one of the individuals received a very significant raise. It was a

40

raise that Human Resources resisted, but my boss skillfully deflected all resistance. Incredibly, Human Resources would've rather hired someone from the outside at the higher pay scale, than to promote someone from within because of the significant percentage increase. It was a bad case of myopia.

After that, the big picture set in. It was a way to reduce expenses. As a result of these promotions in my department and across the country, overtime was vastly reduced if not eliminated.

I was later informed that these individuals who had been reclassified as team leaders were still eligible for overtime as a result of an error in their classification on paper. They were still team leaders, but they were eligible for overtime. I received the information from accounting. I contacted my manager.

> Author to manager: *"I found out from accounting that these employees are still eligible for overtime."*
> Manager: *"I don't care what accounting says, it has to come from Human Resources."*
> Author: *"Maybe you should check."*
> (Note: Manager never checked.)

One year later, an employee—a team leader—complained to Human Resources that he was tired of working overtime and not getting paid for it.

I'll cut to the point.

Human Resources, fearing a lawsuit, contacted all the managers to find out if their team leaders had kept track of their overtime worked for the year and, if not, to estimate it.

Overtime back pay ended up costing the company probably close to $100,000.00.

Incredibly, (I say that a lot don't I?) I later discovered that a few of the other managers had coerced some of the team leaders to reduce their reported overtime hours. Does it never end?!

Incredibly my boss could not recall ever having the conversation with me.

Incredibly the team leaders were reclassified again to ensure that they were not eligible for overtime. All sorts of hoops were jumped through to ensure that job descriptions were drafted in a manner consistent with what a supervisor should probably be doing. Never mind what they actually did, so long as they were classified as exempt from getting paid overtime.

You just can't make this stuff up.

Flexibility

14) Be flexible. A flexible employee is resilient and valuable. Some think that because they are successful, their way is always the best way. This is not the case. This will never be the case. The business world and everything in it is very dynamic; consequently, flexibility and adaptability must be a part of every employee's repertoire.

Author: *"Why can't we do that?"*
Manager: *"It is not the corporate standard."*

Author: *"Then we need to challenge the corporate standard."*

Marines are flexible. They can adapt to the environment and blend in.

Bruce Lee once said, "Be like water." If you cannot adapt your behavior to a situation, you will not succeed. When it came to self-defense, he recognized that flexibility and responsiveness were much more effective than rigidity and choreographed mechanical movements. That, I think, is part of what made him a legend in the martial arts community.

Initiative

15) Employees must exhibit initiative. If you think and act, you will stay ahead. Initiative, tempered with knowledge and experience, will simplify everyone's life and make you a much more effective and valued employee. Employers value employees that do not need to be reminded to do the simplest or most obvious tasks. In my experience, people tend to ignore things in the hopes that someone else will take care of them. No one else takes care of them; consequently, nothing gets accomplished.

Some simple examples of initiative:
- ✓ Clean up after yourself
- ✓ Be on time
- ✓ Help your team
- ✓ If you know your boss needs something, get it done without being asked.
- ✓ Improve your skills

Manager to author: *"Why did you do that without asking?"*
Author: *"It needed to get done."*
Manager: *"Next time check with me."*
Author: *"You pay me to manage, so let me manage."*

Measurements & Reports

16) Apply metrics toward achieving realistic objectives not as a whipping stick. Measure what is needed to maintain control and keep the business moving forward. Numbers can be manipulated; therefore, metrics must be carefully assessed and implemented. Measuring for the sake of measuring wastes time. Be careful of averages because they can distort facts, and be flexible in the use of metrics.

Reports are not necessarily a bad thing because they can inform the uninformed, but reports represent history. When employees have to spend time creating lots of reports in exacting formats, they are not being productive. Managers must balance their perceived need for documented information with actual business requirements, management interest, and productive time available.

One day, one of my direct reports dropped everything and spent half a day preparing a very urgent report for an executive. We sent the e-mail with the information stamped with "read receipt." The manager opened the e-mail and not even five seconds later, my direct report received a thank-you and a "great job." The only problem was that there was no way in the world that information could have been viewed, much less absorbed, in that short amount of time, and of course we never heard about it

44

again. The report was an unforgivable waste of someone's valuable time, all because someone got a bug up his butt somewhere in the hierarchy.

I think companies are paralyzed, paralyzed by the fear of lawsuits; paralyzed by political correctness. As a result, you have lots of rules and reports to "cover thy rear."

Let's talk about the performance-appraisal process. I'm told the process is for the employee. I don't buy it. The process exists to protect the company. Over the years, I have seen appraisal forms from one page in length to more than ten pages to be used in this forced ritual of mental marathoning. Once, I actually sat in my office with some colleagues crying tears because we were laughing so hard at my most recent performance appraisal. It was more like a psychological evaluation. It was so long and ridiculous that it was actually funny.

Employees should know how they are doing throughout the year. Yes, things should be documented–both good and bad, so that there are no ambiguities when someone is being disciplined or rewarded. But, the evaluation process should be a living process, and it shouldn't consume the manager doing it or the employee receiving it.

When it comes to appraisals, I will complete the tedious and monotonous corporate standard, but I deliver my lean version. Why? Because the way I do it is simple, to the point, and genuine. My direct reports know where they stand at all times because I communicate. They know that I am accessible seven days a week if they have any issues or concerns. Employees can talk to me whenever they feel a need, whether I am at work or not. Since there are no surprises, when I deliver the appraisal it is short and to the point. The employees actually appreciate this. I know, I have asked them, and I have often been through the formal process to the point of almost dozing off a few times. I have actually had employees sign their formal performance appraisals without even reading them, which actually goes to show how much value an employee places on these very subjective documents.

> Manager to author: *"The performance review score is not a motivator, it is a measurement. People are motivated when managers honestly share information and develop them. I would not respect a manager who gave me a score that did not reflect my performance."*
> (Note: I do not agree with the first statement.)

I have seen managers spend countless hours trying to come up with the right wording for an appraisal, and depending on how many direct reports exist, the process can take days. This time is lost; time that could be much better spent, maybe even talking to the employee. Talking with employees…what a concept!

> Manager to author: *"You need to change that rating. No one is a five."*
> Author: *"I disagree. This year she was a five. If I could give her a six, I would."*
> Manager: *"If you give a five, that means there is no room for improvement."*
> Author: *"The fact of the matter is she performed at a five level. I know my people."*

The formal once- or twice-yearly performance appraisal should be replaced with a living process that fosters regular and open dialogue with employees through the course of regular activities supported by whatever lean documentation is necessary. Appraisals should be a natural, clean, and simple process for everyone involved. Appraisals should never feel like a visit to the dentist. (My apologies to all dentists)

Author to manager: *"You need to remove that measurement from my appraisal."*
Manager: *"Why?"*
Author: *"Because it is not within my control."*
Manager: *"But everyone else is also being measured on that."*
Author: *"I know, and they don't control it either, but I want it removed from mine. As far as I am concerned, it doesn't exist."*
(Note: The metric was removed.)

The Marines have metrics also, but many are visual. "There is your target; kill it." Go ahead and document that.

Involvement

17) Do not micro manage. Let the team know what is required and then back off. Individuals need to feel they are contributing, not just regurgitating information in a pre-mandated format. Micro managing limits possibilities and causes resentment. Let the results tell the story. I am not suggesting not to be involved, just let employees do their thing. If they can't, then it means the manager did not provide the proper training, guidance, or goals.

Coworker to author: *"You told me what to do. Now let me do it."*

Author to manager: *"Listen, I can't help it that you are bored, but if I am not doing my job to your satisfaction, please let know, and I will make the necessary adjustments. Otherwise, relax."*

Mentoring

18) Be a mentor without being a preacher. There is a difference in someone who honestly mentors and helps another from someone who pushes his views and constantly wants credit and recognition for his interference. A true mentor does not need constant neon lights of praise for her contributions. Helping a colleague or friend is its own reward.

Author to coworker: *"Why did you do that?"*
Coworker: *"You told me to."*
Author: *"Why didn't you question me?"*
Coworker: *"You're my mentor."*
Author: *"Man, I am moved, but please, if you ever think I am heading in the wrong direction, help me to redirect."*

I think having a mentor is an important part of a successful career. I've had individuals throughout my career assist me, but I never had a real mentor. Maybe I am not easily mentored, although I have learned a lot from watching others. If I had to choose someone who influenced me, I would have to say it was my drill instructor in boot camp.

He taught me how to push myself past my weaknesses, lessons that have served me well.

Toward the latter half of my career, I approached an executive I thought I knew pretty well. I came right out and asked him to mentor me, to help me with the polish I had been told I needed. His response:

"I never had a mentor. I think they are a waste of time."

It was an unfortunate opinion on his part. I felt silly, and even though he owed me nothing, my level of respect for him lowered a few notches.

Compromising

19) Never attack the feelings or personality of a person who does not agree with your point of view. Be open-minded. Discuss alternatives. Employees must often be accommodating while remaining responsible.

Manager to author: *"That was a mistake. You need to reprimand that employee."*
Author: *"It was my decision. Leave the employee alone."*

For me, compromising is like adapting in that if I don't have sufficient information or something is not critically important to me, I will adapt to the situation. However, there is a time for talk, and there is a time for action.

Manager to author: *"I learned a long time ago to choose my battles wisely."*
Author: *"But there are so many to choose from."*

Years ago an intern was brought into our department. He was an amiable and intelligent individual, but for some reason he always had something to say to me, not necessarily offensive, but he was a wise guy. One day I had enough, so I went up to him and in a very non-threatening manner I asked if we could speak outside. He agreed. Once outside, I asked him what it was about me that made him react in that fashion toward me. I said that whatever it was, it would be settled right then. He was taken aback and genuinely seemed surprised; the man did not even realize what he was doing, but I never had a problem with him again. There was no compromise.

Higher Education

20) Higher education is very important. But a manager should not get so hung up on titles or degrees that he fails to uncover any hidden gems. Leaders need to take time to get to know employees. Employees should be cultivated to build both competence in the search for results and thinking skills that lead to results and team building.

"With my strongest recommendation, they won't even talk to you without a degree."
Author's friend trying to get him an interview at a pharmaceutical company

-----

"We don't need you. You haven't got through college yet."
Hewlett-Packard executive to Steve Jobs and Steve Wozniak (founders of Apple) (from *The Experts Speak –*

Christopher Cerf and Victor Navasky)

Marines are constantly drilling and practicing, and the best, most disciplined always rise to the top. Success is about preparation. Marines are always prepared. Companies must always prepare, and this readiness begins with investing in the employee.

The Greek philosopher Socrates stated that all knowledge is remembering. I think what he means is that there is no real "new" knowledge. Knowledge is somehow passed on, rediscovered, or even found, but it is always there. Consequently, we are what we think. We are what we learn (or re-learn), so although companies should encourage and provide training, employees must take responsibility for their growth, whether it is through school, on-the-job training, or reading books. Knowledge is there; it just needs to be tapped.

Knowledge

21) Learning is life-long, and wisdom is the application of that learning. Invest in employees and achieve improved margins. Leaders understand that we are a product of our experiences. The more exposure to a variety of environments and the more training we receive, the more we can think creatively, be productive, and recognize opportunity.

"Your writing is a reflection on you, me, and on the department."
Author to employees sent to a writing seminar

I am a classic example. As mentioned earlier, when I started with the company, I knew little. The more I learned and the more I was exposed to various situations, the more effective I became. Simply put, as my mind expanded so did the possibilities. As the possibilities expanded so did my desire for more knowledge (knowledge begets knowledge).

> Manager to author: *"You don't need all this literature."*
> Author: *"It is industry information that keeps me current with changing times."*
> Manager: *"You need more confidence; use your experience."*
> Author: *"It has nothing to do with confidence; it is an investment."*
> Manager: *"If it were your company, would you spend that money?"*
> Author: *"Absolutely."*
> (Note: All subscriptions for everyone were canceled.)

The more you know and the more you can think flexibly, the more valuable you are to an organization. The closer you are to the customer, the more value you bring to the table. What I mean is that if you are generating tangible and measurable value like in sales or a revenue-generating department, it is a good place to be. If you are not, it is a compelling reason to be prepared for the unknown or possible outsourcing.

Bottom line, everyone is expendable, but moneymakers are higher up on the food chain.

Loyalty & Combating Negativity

22) Be loyal. Loyalty requires courage and tenacity. Never set someone up to fail. Never back stab. If someone is

not succeeding in a position, a leader will dig for the reason and colleagues will help. Employees must help each other succeed by identifying the reason for the problems, fixing the cause of problems, or changing the environment that may perpetuate the problem. Management must be engaged.

Loyalty, like leadership, functions best reciprocally; that is top down and bottom up. I have talked to employees who questioned their manager's loyalty to them because of an unpopular decision. I have had to explain that sometimes, no matter what the relationship, the manager must make decisions that will either anger or disappoint employees. It is at these times that the employee-manager relationship is truly tested. Employees develop expectations that are not in line with reality; consequently, the employee-manager relationship is easily damaged. Establishing realistic expectations and consistent, honest, and open communication can help to avoid these relationship breakdowns.

Coworker to author: *"Your great friend has betrayed you."*
Author: *"I know, but he had no choice. He's trying to meet someone else's expectations."*
Coworker: *"You would never do that to someone."*
Author: *"I know."*

I often hear employees criticizing their colleagues or bosses and vice versa–the criticisms…the gossip…the negativity. Now, I am not talking about an occasional comment or vent. What I am talking about is the never-ending blather and groupthink that may begin as an early morning talk-show comment that mushrooms into the evening news and then morphs into a soap opera. It's all poison and a waste of time and energy. Stop it. Do we ever stop to think how all that energy can be channeled toward a more useful conclusion? Negativity gains nothing, nada. Gossip and negativity are momentum-building processes that result in NOTHING. Stay away from them.

> *"He may not be the best communicator or fast on the computer, but he is a hard worker who gets the job done and company man. In today's world, you can't buy that kind of loyalty or commitment."*
Author successfully defending coworker to manager at a personal price

A Marine is loyal. We are loyal to the Corps, to each other, to our country. The Marine Corps nurtures this behavior. The Marine Corps demands this behavior.

Respect & Truth

23) Genuinely respect everyone. Everyone in the organization should be valued. I was once lectured about only being able to work well with people I respect. I have worked hard over the years to change that weakness in my personality and I believe I have been successful by developing acceptance. But this acceptance is tempered by distinguishing between those who can't and those who won't.

If someone is not performing, I will let him or her know about it. We need to respect each other enough to speak the truth and move on. But be aware, speaking the truth can be a hazard to some relationships. Not everyone wants to hear the truth. Everyone searches for truth, but not everyone really wants it, especially when truth and self-perception are at odds.

> Employee: *"You are very intense."*
> Author: *"I'm sorry . . . really. You just need to get to know me."*

> Employee: *"I deserved that award."*
> Author: *"Why?"*
> Employee: *"I have been here a long time, and I deserve it."*
> Author: *"You have been here a long time and you do good work . . . when you want to. You are far from consistent. The person who received the award is consistently very good."*

Uncovering truth is a work in process for the unpretentious. Even experts on "things" disagree on truth within their areas of expertise because of their unique experiences and perceptions. Truth can be found only by being aware of our self-imposed limitations on how we think or view our surroundings. Believe me, it is not easy, but it can be accomplished and it must be practiced to maintain an active state of alertness.

Some things are black and white. Many times things are gray. We must resist the tendency to jump to conclusions.

> Manager to author: *"Our customers love our quality."*
> Author: *"How do you know?"*
> Manager: *"We send out surveys."*
> Author: *"What do you do with the non-responses?"*
> Manager: *"We count them as favorable responses."*

55

Relationships

24) Build true relationships without favoritism. A network of dependable relationships, at various levels, will ensure that the manager is well informed and can get things done, but do not use people. Relationships are very important and can greatly enhance business environments.

Define success in your own terms, but not at the expense of anyone else. The saying "What goes around comes around" is valid. The consequences to the user, backstabber, or egotist may or may not be immediate, but there are consequences for everything.

> *"Stop helping them. They just use you."*
> Coworker to author

A long-time employee, as he climbed the corporate ladder, alienated many people. For this individual, it was his way or no way. When business conditions changed and a newly developed position he had attained was eliminated, no one lifted a hand to help him. He had to leave the organization.

The failure in this case was two-fold.

First, this individual's management accepted his tactics while those tactics furthered their objectives. No one ever bothered to counsel him or his employees.

Second, this manager did not build relationships. He was a dictator, pure and simple. It took years, but his treatment of others caught up to him.

Family At Work

25) Treat employees like family. At work, my crew is like an extended family. Not everyone responds to that kind of environment, but those who do will be valuable allies throughout a career. I have learned that, for the most part, true relationships can be built inside or outside of the workplace, and in turn the workplace becomes a better and more productive place. The reason is that when there is a relationship, individuals want to help each other; consequently, the effort is real, not just an obligation of labor with minimal contribution and effort. As a result, there is an understanding and commitment between employees that no dollar could buy.

Just as important, individuals who blur the line between business and personal relations must be immediately corrected. Once again, honest communication is the key.

"The only thing that keeps me here is you and the team that we've built."
Coworker to author as the company changed, not for the better

Marines are a family. It is interesting to watch Marines, who know nothing about each other, strike up a conversation when one realizes that both have served. I am not sure how to explain it, other than the bond that is forged from the common experience of boot camp and having served in the military.

I would like to think that over the years I made some valuable contributions to my company by eliminating waste, speeding up processes, and optimizing costs. These accomplishments are a result of teamwork. But for me, my biggest achievement and validation of the principles I am presenting in this manifesto occurred on an October afternoon in 2003.

A few people from my department attended an operations conference where performance awards and recognition were given to some of the attendees. I was not mentioned. After the conference, members of my team approached me and voiced their dismay. I basically told them that it was to be expected, considering the strained relationship between my boss and me. I told them not to sweat it and to just enjoy the conference, but they were really bothered.

After the conference, and unknown to me at the time, they drafted a letter and sent it to my immediate manager voicing their disappointment. They took this action at professional risk to themselves. My manager then scheduled a conference call with these individuals to discuss their concerns.

As it turns out, he never addressed their concerns. He attempted only to validate his position and why the other people received their awards. My team was further disillusioned, but wisely said nothing.

My manager never mentioned this incident to me, and I am not surprised. But, he did succeed in solidifying my team's perception of "us versus them."

My coworkers and I had built a strong and solid team and we were a family. A bond like that is not easily broken by empty words or veiled threats from others.

To ensure that I was not allowing myself to twist the memory of those events, the individuals who were involved in the incident acknowledged and approved what you just read.

Change

26) "Never underestimate the power to change yourself, and never overestimate the power to change others." A waitress at a restaurant said that to me, and it is something to live by.

It is very important to understand that we must embrace change. However, change is best coming from the inside when we recognize the need and act on it, as opposed to having change imposed on us.

Author: "*What's with all the red marks?*"
Manager: "*Grammatical errors. You need to pay attention.*"
Author: "*This is ridiculous . . . but I'll work on it.*"

Manager: "*What's this?*"
Author: "*Grammatical errors.*"
Manager: "*That's my writing style, so it's acceptable.*"

I've had people try to change me. It does not work. Individuals change to the extent that change is not inconsistent with their core self. Forced change is emotionally and mentally disruptive–morale will suffer.

I have changed and evolved, but much of my growth has been at my discretion and according to my managed environment. I do wish I had known ten years ago what I know today because I now recognize that back then, I reacted to my environment as opposed to taking control and managing my environment. Today, I work on being proactive.

I once worked with a colleague who tried to fit into a group of employees when there was tangible conflict between the group's behavior and the individuals' beliefs. Job preservation drove him. While most of the other followers were very successful, he lost weight and had constant stomach problems. He was not allowed to be himself. I met with him almost a year after he had left the organization for other opportunities, and he was healthy as a horse. He gained weight, and he was relaxed. I barely recognized him. This individual could not be forced to change into something that was not within him, and it was only after he changed his environment that he was able to really smile again.

> Coworker to author: *"Every time I have to meet with my boss, I get the shits."*

Understanding

27) Understand and accept differences in others. Stephen Covey, in *The Seven Habits of Highly Effective People*, wrote, "Seek to understand before being understood." (I highly recommend his book) One of my own general beliefs is that although I may not know it all, through others my ability to understand is strengthened.

> Author to coworker: *"Please help me understand."*

I was having a performance problem with an employee. After weeks of counseling, I was ready to initiate the steps

60

necessary to permanently correct the behavior–he was on his way out. I knew this individual had great potential, so I approached him as a friend and asked him to confide in me. He did, and I understood better what was causing the erratic behavior. I worked with him, he got past a bad period in his life, and he was well on his way to being successful. All it took was patience and understanding.

Author to coworker: *"You need to talk to me now!"*

Leaders must reach beyond themselves. Leaders are caregivers. They are consultants and psychologists. They are the magnet and the glue that can bring and hold people together. It's the human side of management. I am not saying a leader has to be wishy-washy or weak; that is not the intent. I have released a few employees for various reasons, but in all cases with patience and understanding. No one, I venture, was ever caught by surprise.

The other day, someone asked me to describe my role as a manager. "I am a facilitator," was my answer, but I wear many hats.

"Just know from afar I wish I had a boss like you. I used to at another company, and you remind me of my boss there, always there, always in tune with his people, caring, and totally involved, sometimes unfortunately at his expense."
Coworker to author

Trust

28) Trust is the cornerstone of any relationship, whether

personal or professional. If there is no trust, there will be no success.

In my area of responsibility, I can go away for weeks and not worry that the department will fall apart. It was not always that way. But, by leading in the right fashion and building relations, my team has become reliable, confident, and very productive. I did not always know how to manage, and I still have much to learn, but by working together and accepting that I do not know it all, my direct reports and I learned from each other. We became a very cohesive group.

Even though we are a trusted and cohesive group, I have learned to listen, and as a result, I learned that there are always a few whose loyalty could come into question if things got heated. Those are the individuals who bend with the wind, and those are the ones you trust with caution. But it is not always their fault. People like that sometimes have good intentions, but fear drives them to act in certain ways.

I have also been associated with a few managers who, face to face, use their words to create an aura of strength and conviction. I have witnessed these managers crumble in the face of the slightest challenge from management or with the slightest stress. These types of individuals say one thing and behave or do things completely opposite from their public persona. They are eventually found out by employees and treated accordingly, with little respect and absolutely no trust.

Manager to author: *"If I ever went into battle, I would want you by my side."*

That is the kind of trust and loyalty that strengthens relationships and unfortunately seems to be in very short supply.

Trust must be built—it is earned.

> Author: *"I cannot do that."*
> Manager: *"Why?"*
> Author: *"Because I gave my word to the customer that I would never do that."*
> Manager: *"But it's no big deal."*
> Author: *"I'm sorry. I will not do it unless we get the customer's approval first."*

In the Marines trust is developed and earned during training. We must trust our fellow Marines to do right by us—cover our backs; otherwise, we could be killed

Teamwork requires trust.

One day I received a call from an employee who once reported to me. He needed to vent. Apparently his immediate manager scheduled a team conference call to discuss certain issues and to solicit feedback. Unknown to everyone on the conference call except the manager, the executive in charge of the department was listening in on the conference call. He didn't reveal himself until later in the call, after honest and open discussions had taken place, and then only to chastise the employees who spoke up. Needless to say, the employee who called me was shocked at his manager's betrayal, and the manager lost whatever credibility he had. Trust never to be regained.

Humility

29) Be humble. Do not get so hung up on your perceived abilities that you do not solicit opinions or counsel on matters that impact other employees or the organization.

Never forget that ultimately the organization is a team, like in a relay race. Individual departments represent sections of the race that must work in unison to achieve the desired objective.

> *"I really hope you start to get it."*
> Manager to author
>
> ---
>
> *"You can't just shit on people."*
> Author to manager

The Marine Corps is composed of many unique individuals who are forged into a team. There is always someone who is smarter, works harder, runs longer.

Be strong and be humble because humility inspires.

Our operations manager came up with an idea. He decided that he would try to create a revenue-generating department from a department that was pure overhead. Conceptually, it was a good idea, but his methodology was shaky at best.

I was literally being forced to become a salesperson for a service that did not yet exist. I was told I had to come up with a customer list and a method to track commissions and sales. These expectations were even added to my performance measures. All a sudden, without any warning or discussion, I was being measured on something I had never done before or been trained to do; not that selling should be a big deal. But in my mind, my job was one or the other, not both. You can't be expected to be in two places, being successful at two completely different functions, at once. It violates the principal of focus. And of course I was told I needed to think "out of the box." For the record, I came to hate that phrase.

If the project had taken off, I think I could have done a good job, but not under the conditions that we worked in. There needed to be some major paradigm changes, and I knew that would never happen. This story should stop here, but as usual, it gets better.

I was told to attend what was to be a training session.

> Author to colleague: *"Who is doing the training?"*
> Colleague: *"Our manager."*
> Author: *"How is that possible? He has never sold a thing in his life."*

I booked my ticket to the next adventure, and wouldn't you know it, I became very ill midway through the training. I don't know why I got sick, but I have a suspicion.

I am a firm believer in the "right authority." Hey, just because someone is a great basketball player does not make him a great baseball or football player. It seems pretty simple to me. If you do think you are multitalented, you better have the credentials to back it up.

I suspect that my predisposition about the "right authority" led my mind and body to revolt. It was incredibly difficult to sit through those sessions. It made me ill. Through all the haze the only thing I learned, or think I was supposed to learn, was that if prospects did not recognize our product as an enhancement to their business, they were not that bright. Sounds like a winning recipe for sales success, don't you think?

Now I'm no salesperson, but I do know that successful salesmanship requires some understand of the human psyche, and for me, high-pressure sales don't work. It does not matter whether I want or need a product or service, when faced with a high-pressure pitch, an automatic no will result.

According to a *Harvard Business Review* magazine article (July-August 2006), a man name Joe Girard holds the Guinness Record for being the world's best salesman. He sold 13,001 individual cars over the course of fifteen years, and he did it by loving his customers and showing them respect. It was all about relationships. Mr. Girard is now a speaker on the subject of sales. He has the credentials.

The world's shortest sales course:
Know their business
Know your stuff
(*Bits and Pieces*, motivational magazine)

There is an extreme professional danger in having management with too much time on its hands. The employees become guinea pigs.

Escalating Commitment

30) Never be guilty of following a failing course of action, also known as the escalating commitment. If a mistake

is made, admit it and learn from it. Change course if need be, but do not attempt to hide or pass off your mistake. Everyone will see through you. The manager who attempts to save face will never recover in the eyes of employees. A strong leader will not hesitate to apologize, change course, and move on.

I was invited to participate in a project that would change our organization. I recognized the seeds of inadequate preparation and potential disaster because of previous experience in similar projects. I was so concerned about the impending waste of time and money that I wrote a letter to the chief executive officer informing him, very respectfully, that we were embarking on a mission using old methods that were proven not to work. I did not sleep for a couple of nights wondering what his reaction would be, wondering how I would survive what some considered an act of lunacy. As it turned out, he was very understanding, but in the final analysis concluded, "We have done way too much work on this process to start over with a new one."

The results of the project were much less than satisfying, but it was completed on time, and therefore was considered a success. Efficiency and effectiveness were compromised for speed and some level of comfort or convenience. They basically took a square peg and made it fit into a round hole. It was forced through, and it would never really fit.

"Previous projects have been plagued with lack of receptiveness to communication, role ambiguities (even with the consultants, in some cases), inadequate training (from a user perspective), and functional isolationism, just to name a few . . ." Author communication to CEO

67

Note: I do not know what goes on in the executive offices or why some decisions are made. Public companies have pressures that I can only begin to imagine, but I often shake my head in disbelief at the decisions that are passed down.

Announcement to project team: *"Congratulations on the successful completion of the project."*

Author: *"Let the games begin."*

Manager to author: *"They just set the company back five to ten years."*

Common Sense

31) Employees must possess and use common sense. Rules and guidelines are required, but sometimes a rule or policy must be modified or changed to suit a specific situation. In business as in life, change is constant, exceptions are the rule, and human propensities cannot always be predicted.

If policy cannot be modified to suit specific circumstances in an ever changing business and technological world, opportunities may be missed. Business strategy and operations must be balanced with common sense. Written rules and policies must be responsive not restrictive.

Leaders must be able to reason.

Common sense is critical in an ever-changing world. The manager who does not have common sense must face it and then proceed to surround him or herself with it. This step would require a long look in the mirror, and not just to dress up.

Author to colleague: *"You're not promoting the business; you are defending a lifestyle. You need to make changes."*

Manager to author: *"The policy is that all customers are treated in this particular fashion."*
Author: *"But not all customers fall into that category. The process hurts good customers and needs to be modified."*
Manager: *"It's the policy."*

The Marines must master common sense to adapt to fluid conditions.

Rules

32) Do not hide behind rules. I have known managers who love to break the rules if it furthers their objectives; however, the same managers have been heard to say to other employees that something cannot be done because it is against the rules. How convenient.

Author to manager: *"You guys are funny. You are doing the very same thing that you said that other employee should be fired for. How does that work?"*
Manager: *"You're right, but I am only doing what I am told to do."*
Author: *"How convenient!"*

We are not supposed to wear jeans to work. For operations people, I don't understand the big deal; there is no customer contact. A decent (no holes or stains) pair of jeans with shoes or boots and a polo shirt can make a nice appearance. But we did have a "Hawaiian shirt day" once a month. So, one Friday I wore jeans, thinking no one would notice. One minute everything was fine, when suddenly, I found myself standing in front of the vice president getting a lecture on the company policy against jeans. The killer here is that he had on a Hawaiian shirt because it happened to be "Hawaiian shirt day." He looked real silly behind the big oak desk, sitting back in his big leather chair, giving me a big lecture in his big, floppy Hawaiian shirt. I realize I broke policy, but the irony of the whole thing still makes me smile. It was one of those "you can't be serious" moments.

Human Resources

33) Corporations must make human resources a real, empowered department that truly has the best interest of the employee at heart. Part of HR's responsibility, in addition to mapping out benefits and careers, should be to keep their finger on the pulse of employee morale—although not just to provide lip service. Consistency across the organization is important to build the corporate foundation and ensure that local management is fair and impartial.

Jack Welch, among many great suggestions and observations in his books, recommends elevating HR to very important and meaningful levels. Executives, take heed.

Management needs policing. The executive or manager's prerogative to rule as he sees fit is a myth. For me, it stops here. It stops now. Impartiality, fairness, and sensitivity must be demanded and enforced at all levels of the organization.

"There is no policy against bad management."
Human Resource manager to author

We were once an organization where employees did not leave. It was a good place to be. Over the years we morphed into an organization where employees prayed for an opportunity to leave–anything just to get out.

In many cases employees left because of management tactics, many of which have been described in this writing. In a few cases, employees that were being laid off sacrificed their severance packages when an opportunity to exit arose. If walking away from a package does not speak volumes . . .

You would think flags would go up–something was wrong; however, Human Resources was nowhere to be found. The corporate executive leadership was oblivious to their surroundings.

As we neared the end of our tenure where I worked, a coworker informed me that the company had outsourced the function of employment referrals. She expressed serious reservations about the process.

If a potential employer wanted to verify a candidate's past employment and salary with this company, the potential employer would have to log on to a Web site and pay a fee to obtain the information. I don't know about anyone else, but I find that method ridiculous.

Upon learning of this requirement, many potential employers would probably lose interest and not pursue a candidate. Why place the candidate at risk?

> Author to H.R. manager: *"I don't have your experience, but why on earth would this company even remotely think of creating a situation that could potentially jeopardize an ex-employee's opportunity for employment?"*
> HR manager: *"To be frank with you, I don't have a good answer. Please let them know that they can call me, but I won't verify salary without a written request."*

It is what it is . . .

Compensation

34) Companies must pay well and reward exceptional performance when it occurs. Do not use professional surveys to justify limits on compensation. I understand that there must be guidelines and thresholds, but without reward there is no incentive. An employee who feels cheated or underappreciated will not be productive. Some employees who feel cheated or underappreciated will cheat management at every opportunity. It is human nature, and I have seen it happen.

"The United States has the best process of all operating companies."
Colleague from overseas on one of the author's operations

Remember, individuals feel they are owed something, so they will seek to compensate themselves if they do not think the company is doing it appropriately. Employees sometimes forget that they have a choice to either improve their skills or leave the organization, but to do this they have to "unlazify"; otherwise, it doesn't happen. Unfortunately, they continue to torture themselves.

To make up for any perceived wrong, some employees may practice "perceptual redress," and it can take many forms. An example would be an employee who suddenly develops sticky fingers, begins overextending his breaks or lunches, begins arriving late, or has sudden excessive absences. I call it perceptual redress because of the illusory belief that some kind of payback has been exacted, when in reality, all that has occurred is a manifestation of a weakened moral foundation.

The solution is to pay well and treat employees as partners in the business.

> Author: "*This employee needs a bonus.*"
> Manager: "*Why?*"
> Author: "*Because she did a great job. Just look at the numbers.*"
> Manager: "*That is her job.*"
> Author: "*Anyone can do the job. It's the level of performance unique to this person that we are rewarding.*"

I had a couple of employees who were excellent at what they did. They received all kinds of praise from management and executives not only for results, but also for having a team attitude. One year those employees did not receive pay increases because they were "maxed out." These individuals were hurt and crushed. They put in lots of time, and the jobs they did saved the organization tons of money—in the millions. These savings were easily quantifiable. None of these facts mattered to management because of a silly limitation called a pay-grade and salary scale.

I worked with these individuals to show them that they were highly valued, but the damage to morale was done, and it was permanent. It wasn't just that the employees did not receive increases; it was the cavalier attitude of management that went something like this: "If they don't like it, they need to leave or change jobs."

The result was predictable. The jobs were still getting completed, but it was amazing how employees can time their arrival to work within seconds of their start time and how fast the computer can be shut off at the official end of a workday. There was a very noticeable change in the employees' demeanor, and I can't say that I blame them.

Bonus Plans

35) Be vigilant with the bonus plan. A bonus plan not properly administered and not cross-business oriented can lead people to play games with numbers. Money can challenge the ethics of almost anyone. The trick, and I know it's not easy, is not to become dependent on a bonus unless you are in a plan where the bonus is a significant factor in salary, like sales. The real solution is not letting money control you. I repeat, do not let money control you.

See Appendix B for thoughts on money and self-control.

> Author to employee: *"Your standby pay and your overtime pay are not guaranteed. They can disappear any day, so do not become dependent on them."*
> Employee: *"That's easier said than done, I have bills to pay."*
> (Note: Standby pay and overtime were eliminated)

In my ten years of receiving bonuses, I have never once made a decision driven by consideration for an incentive. I chose my job, it did not choose me; thus, I work to the best of my abilities and then some. I treat corporate funds like I would treat my own. To me, the bonus plan is just a benefit of being in management. If I do my job the best that I can, the money should flow, at least that was what I thought. It doesn't work that way. You have to go after what you want.

> Manager to author: *"You don't understand. They don't do it because it is not part of their incentive."*
> Author: *"That's bull! Someone just needs to grow some balls and really manage for once. You don't need to incent common sense."*

I am not in finance, but there must be a more effective way to manage bonuses, and, more importantly, budgets. Budgets should not be an encumbrance and should not encourage needless spending, but that is exactly what happens because of the way they are created and managed. A friend once said to me "Tell me your silly rules, and I'll play your silly games." That statement pretty much sums up the budget process.

Budgets should have flexibility built into them and should encourage thinking. I've read about companies that use creative methods like percentages for tracking and monitoring spending to allow for some of this flexibility. After reading about the concept, I brought it to the attention of our business managers, and I was told that it would take too much effort and change, and the timing was just not right. It never is.

> Manager to author: *"We have got to spend what's left; otherwise, they'll reduce the budget for next year."*
> Comment to author after resisting a $70,000.00 purchase toward the end of the year

-----

> Manager to author: *"Make sure those transactions are completed before the end of the month."*
> Author: *"But they are not complete."*
> Manager: *"Just close out the transaction. We must meet the numbers. The physical part can take place later."*

Quality Initiatives

36) Be cautious with the various business solutions being marketed. Some processes or proposed solutions are passing trends and some are not. Try to find the best ideas and mold them to organizational requirements. An example of this would be Six Sigma. Six Sigma can be powerful, but it also keeps many people employed in consulting and in training. Six Sigma should be going on in companies all the time;

management and employees should always strive to drive out inefficiencies. Is this a new concept?!

The efficiency and effectiveness of the business should not be outsourced and should not be complicated. Dozens of forms and statistics are not required to get a job done. Make Six Sigma or simply controlled quality a core competency, not a special project. Keep things simple. Keep things lean.

Manager to author: *"They better find some savings; otherwise, they can't justify her (*vice president of Six Sigma*) salary."*

One important catch regarding any process improvement project is that a company must ensure the obvious obstacles have been overcome. These smaller projects can be referred to as "low-hanging fruit." Only after harvesting your low-hanging fruit can any project success be realistically measured in terms of any payback associated with it. For example, it might be tempting to just throw Six Sigma at a problem and then rave about all the success, but it is wrong and misleading if the problem is a fairly obvious one that can be resolved by management intervention and employee involvement.

Here is a curious situation. The company hires an executive to initiate quality control projects (it pays the individual six figures as it is laying off employees). What the company executives do not realize or understand is that there is so much "low-hanging fruit" that a rat would never starve.

Now this individual initiates all sorts of projects (remember the low-hanging fruit) and is hailed as some kind of hero. These projects take time and deep involvement by management and selected employees. There is training, presentations, and all sorts of documentation that must be completed at a significant cost to the company.

What was everyone doing prior to the "quality initiative," and are our customers any better off? The evidence indicates that the skipper(s) were asleep at the helm and that customers are no better off.

> Manager to author: *"I was told we need to come up with a Six Sigma project."*
> Author: *"Hold on while I pull one out of my ass (OOMA). If I can come up with one that easily, then it's not a Six Sigma."*
> Manager: *"Let's just get it over with."*

When they first introduced ISO (International Standards Organization) into the organization, I thought it was a joke. It wasn't.

I was convinced that whoever came up with the idea must have been laughing all the way to the bank. We actually paid money to have someone come in and make sure that processes were documented. Then we placed the ISO emblem on our business cards to prove to potential customers that we had documented processes and procedures–never mind whether they were good or bad. To make matters worse, individuals who knew nothing of the business completed the audits! I never once heard of any increase in revenue, customers, or quality because we were ISO certified, but we spent a lot of time and money on ISO.

Whatever happened to management's responsibility to deliver quality?

Consultants

37) Manage consultants. If consultants are required (and sometimes they are), first ensure that all internal resources have been exhausted, and then know what is specifically needed. Never let an outsider drive the business. Consultants give advice; company management drives. Regardless of his expertise, no individual consultant knows it all; therefore, serious consideration must be given to all decisions in light of the fact that other opinions exist. From a business perspective, when a manager comes to a fork in the road a choice must be made based on the available information, and sometimes there is no turning back. Managers must dig for the information leading to the best available path and take nothing at face value.

During one project for a systems upgrade, I was researching system capabilities to see what improvements were available. I thought we had not been given enough information or proper time for preparation, so I did some exploration with transactions and reporting methods. I came across a function that I felt very strongly would improve our efficiency. I mentioned it to the consultant, and he refused to even look at it. He told me, "It's not in the scope of our charter for this implementation."

I responded, *"Scope, my ass. We need this function, and you will configure it."*

We got the function configured.

I used to think consultants were an operations panacea. I have learned that consultants can fill a knowledge gap in the organization, but they must be managed and challenged. There are no panaceas.

See Appendix C for some thoughts on project management.

Cause and Effect

38) An effective manager will question everything. In business, as in life, not everything is as it first seems. The world is intricate and intertwined by diverse possibilities. Managers must choose to question the world around them because individuals have their own take on situations. These perceptions are formed as a result of all our past experiences and how we process them in our minds and apply them to new situations. Rarely, if ever, are the facts simple. Dig for the truth. Understanding cause and effect takes effort; it is not easy, and it often takes work. See appendix D for project blunders as a result of not asking questions.

Manager to author: *"Next time I would appreciate it if you gave me an opportunity to address your concerns."*
Author: *"I am truly sorry. They report to you. I thought you were in on the lunacy."*

Coworker to author: *"He was right about this particular systems transaction."*
Author: *"Yes, but tread softly. They are not sure about anything out there."*
Coworker: *"Even a half-blind squirrel can find a French fry once in while."*

Reflection

39) A leader must be introspective. Reflection leads to personal growth.

She must possess the ability to see through an individual's comments or actions. I have been in meetings where I was the only one voicing an opinion. Even though others shared my beliefs, they did not stand up for themselves. Those employees simply went on delivering what was expected of them, no matter how ridiculous, and hating what they did. In this environment, every Sunday evening was the threshold of hell.

> Author to colleague(s): "*I gave you the opportunity to speak up. Why didn't you back me up?*"
> Colleague: "*I'm sorry. It's just not worth it.*"

A manager must be able to read others. He shouldn't blindly accept that because his requests are completed, everything is great. This awareness can't be achieved without first looking inward.

In one of his movies, Clint Eastwood said, "A man's got to know his limitations." I can add to that "and then try to overcome them."

In boot camp, I was placed in leadership positions, and I did not always succeed. Why? Upon reflection, it was clear that I wasn't ready to lead.

I was once given the honor of leading the platoon. Carrying our platoon flag, I confidently marched in front, flag waving proudly above me, and then it happened.

While the platoon was marching straight, I apparently
was not. It suddenly occurred to me that I was standing all
by my lonesome, and everyone else was probably
wondering, "Where the hell is this guy going?" Needless to
say, I did not hold that position for long.

Today I may not be able to march a straight line–God
only knows, keep a compass away from me–but give me
an objective, and my team will become closer and
stronger in its pursuit. We will reach our objective, and if
there is any doubt, I have no problem asking for
assistance. There is nothing wrong in seeking help or
leveraging other resources that complement a current
skill or resource limitation.

> Coworker to author: *"I'm not sure how to handle
> this."*
> Author to coworker: *"Do the right thing, not just
> when it's convenient, and you can't go wrong."*

Leadership Duality

40) A leader must be capable of being led, regardless of the
source. I have practiced this all my life by questioning
things, not out of disrespect, but out of a desire to
understand, learn, and weed out the obviously irrelevant.
It is part of the on-going learning experience. Managers
should insist on being challenged. Employees should not
mind being challenged–it strengthens development.

> Author to manager: *"The department has an image
> problem that we must correct."*
> Manager to author: *"There is no problem."*
> Note: Department was dismantled; so was the executive

in charge.

There have been a few instances where I tried very hard to help a manager or executive see the bigger picture from a relations and operations standpoint, not from a business standpoint or profit and loss position. Sometimes people are blinded by their own hubris and ambition, and so the saying "cannot see the forest for the trees" applies.

"The mind's eyes begin to see clearly when the outer eyes grow dim." Greek philosopher Socrates

The inability of these people to adapt their behavior to changing circumstances resulted in consequences such as loss of jobs, loss of control, and loss of credibility. Although the solutions to their problems were not solely in my hands or my counsel, certain negative outcomes might have been avoided if they opened their minds and hearts to the possibilities.

"...We desperately need your vision, not someone else's opinion."
Author to manager

Clients

41) Never, ever cheat your customers. Employees must build customer relationships with universally acceptable and agreeable terms. I do not buy into the "customer is always right" mentality, but never lose sight of the fact that without the customer, the business ceases to exist. Without question, the customer must always be treated honestly and with exceptional service and consideration– again, exceptional service and consideration. Welcome

83

and embrace the customer. Customers are your future.

In my environment, I define a customer as everyone we deal with, whether internal or external. On my team there is one phrase that can get you in trouble, and that is "It's not my job." I don't want to hear it. We get phone calls for all sorts of reasons, and no one gets the runaround. If we don't know the answer to something, we'll find out. If we don't know who to forward something to, we'll find out. Good service is all about building relations and trust. My intent is not to build an image, but to inspire a sense of urgency in everything we do.

Employee from another department: *"Not sure what to do. I can't get a hold of anyone . . ."*
Author: *"Take care of the customer first. We'll address the details tomorrow."*

Culture

42) A strong corporate culture is important. Without culture there is no sense of belonging and no sense of purpose, other than getting the job done. Success may come, but it will not be all that it could be. In the right organizational atmosphere, morale is just as important as profit. Strong leaders understand that individual feeling of belonging and ownership will drive employees to excel.

In the right atmosphere, culture isn't defined by policy...it just is.

"We've been practicing these values long before they

came along."
Employee to author after new executive management
created and published core values

Early on in my career, we had no mission statement or
values statement–the political correctness movement was in
its infancy–but every employee somehow understood what
was expected, what needed to be done, and in most cases,
how to get there. In hindsight, this behavior resonated from
one man, our then CEO. It was a culture of service and
performance. This service and performance philosophy was
lost on the organization when our original CEO retired.

Everything starts at the top.

Coworker: *"They're going to miss us when we're gone.
They're going to feel it big time."*
Author: *"No, they won't."*
Coworker: *"Why do you say that?"*
Author: *"Because before us, they survived. They were
satisfied with less-than-average results, and in some
cases, content with no results, just spinning their
wheels. We make more work and create confusion by
pointing out the obvious, by trying to do the right thing.
So trust me . . . we won't be missed."*
Coworker: *"I guess you're right . . . unbelievable!"*
(Note: This conversation took place after we were
informed of impending layoffs)

Employee as an Asset

43) Employees are the most important assets of a business.
Not all employees are valued assets, only the right
employees who embrace these principles. Leaders must

create an environment that revolves around not only business strategy and objectives, but also around their employees. Most employees who believe in what they do, believe they are valued, and believe they share a sense of purpose will reach past mediocrity. Employees must believe and trust in their organization and their management for the business to truly prosper.

Only once have I come across a manager who was a strong proponent of ongoing learning to increase employees' contributions, to make them working assets. This individual's zeal often crossed over to the extreme, and it created problems with his applications, but his influence in that area for his department was important to the organization. It's too bad that a balance of his method and desire was never achieved. For me, it was a case of digging deep to find the really good when the surface was not so great- and there was a lot of good to be found.

> Author to manager: *"I'm just not a good student."*
> Manager to author: *"Neither am I, and I did it. Once you have your degree, no one can take it away from you."*

Balance

44) Leaders must be vigilant of the quality of work life for their employees and themselves. The whole work-life thing has been analyzed and "buzz worded" to death, but there is legitimacy to it. Long hours should not be the norm; they should be the exception. There will be times when long hours are required, and in those situations the employee needs to be shown

appreciation. As you climb the corporate ladder and gain responsibility, hours and salaries increase, but, you must always strive for balance.

I was once guilty of thinking long hours were part of the job, long before I got into management. I missed out on a lot in my personal life because of my misguided notion. The employee and business relationship must be reciprocal and it must be balanced.

I believe balance is a required step prior to achieving success. A *Harvard Business Review* (February 2004) article suggests that enduring success is composed of four components:
1) Happiness–feeling good about yourself and your life
2) Achievement–satisfaction with accomplishments
3) Significance–positive impact within your circle of influence
4) Legacy–mentoring of others

This is a dynamic, interdependent framework that revolves around living a meaningful life, and you cannot live a meaningful life without prioritizing certain aspects of it. It is very simple to lose balance without an occasional review of your priorities in relation to the four components of enduring success.

Do NOT make the mistake, as I did, of equating work with your identity or sense of purpose. I saw a wristwatch ad featuring John Travolta in *Men's Health* magazine. The headline read, "Profession: Pilot, Career: Actor." For some reason, the ad resonated with me, and it helps explain what I am trying to say.

"What the hell are you doing!?"
The author chasing after his wife as she throws the pager out the front door

---

Author to manager: *"I don't understand the need for continually driving employees into the ground. They are not machines."*
Manager: *"I don't care. I want them working ten to twelve hours a day."*

Human nature is sometimes funny and often fickle. We can be like animals in the wild–unpredictable–and management is clueless to this fact. A coworker worked very hard. He came into work early and always left late. He often worked on weekends. He needed balance. This man was productive and a company man, and I, of course, gave him plenty of latitude. Then one day, new management came in and started to demand things. The new managers set expectations. They wanted time measured for all sorts of functions. Latitude all but vanished, but we did this employee a favor. Management found balance for him. No more coming in early, no more staying late. No more volunteering for anything. This individual did his thing out of some sense of personal pride, ownership, and commitment—because he wanted to. When choice was removed; his sense of ownership was removed.

One final thought. After we had received notice of the impending plant closure, I was speaking with a high-level manager who was on the road to retirement. During the conversation, I mentioned how for the first time in twenty years I had taken more than one week's vacation at one time. I mentioned that, in the past, I had always either carried over vacation, or actually lost time because I could never find the time to get away. He looked at me and said, *"And look where it got you!"*

He was right.

Dignity & Courage

45) Never sacrifice dignity out of fear or intimidation. We must be true to ourselves; otherwise, sincerity becomes expedient.

Have the mental and physical courage to stand up for yourself and for others, to be different when different feels right- to do the right thing.

I have been through many ups and downs, and on occasion my self-esteem and dignity have been challenged, but I always bounce back. I am in control, even when others have tried to wrestle control from me. Control is a state of mind. It is a decision.

> Manager to author: *"Let's step over here to the bar and have a drink."*
> Author: *"Sure."*
> Manager: *"I have a question. What do you have against me?"*
> Author: *"You're a prick."*
> (Note: After further discussion there was understanding, and the author and the manager became friends.)

One day in boot camp, we were practicing a marching drill

when a platoon of female Marines marched by. I looked without turning my head. I didn't know my eyeballs could rotate so far left. When we got back to the barracks the drill instructor wanted to know who looked at the women. "Step forward," he demanded.

I thought, "Crap ... what should I do?" I envisioned myself doing pushups for hours, so, unfortunately, I stayed put when, to my astonishment, most of the platoon stepped forward. It was a seriously bad decision on my part. The only thought I had when the drill instructor rushed over to me was, "Oh-Oh." I knew I was in trouble.

"What... are you queer?" he demanded spit spraying into my cringing face, finger shoved into and almost through my chest. Every experience is a lesson. Have the courage to always be accountable.

Dependability

46) Be dependable. If you want any credibility whatsoever, then you must always do what you say you will do or what you commit to doing. Dependability is one of those priceless traits. When you are dependable, you are the go-to person in almost all important projects or assignments, and you will go the extra mile.

Get the job done, no excuses, and you will succeed so long as you don't rest on your successes.

Manager to author: *"We need you on another project."*
Author: *"Not again!"*
Manager: *"We know that we can count on you."*

Clones

47) Leaders need to understand that not everyone has the same abilities or habits. Diversity is not a bad thing, so long as employees try their best and achieve results. Managers should not try to clone themselves or their best employees. No one wants to work with parrots or robots.

Author to coworker: *"You need to get a personality."*

At one point I had a manager who was very organized and controlling. For example, he insisted that presentations from various managers look the same, even down to the outline. The request really wasn't a big deal, but it made for a stifling presentation that lacked creativity.

I had to draw the line. The manager had acquired nice shirts for us with the corporate logo. He told us to wear them to meetings. I was fine with that request until he told us to wear the same colored or light-colored pants. That was part of the problem for me; we were always told what to do, never really asked. Again the rebel in me surfaced. I felt that the demand, in a line of many, was over the top. Never mind that I would've had to buy the pants. I did not carry out the order.

Passion

48) Leaders should display passion. Passion is uplifting. Passionate and self-effacing leaders are approachable, inspiring. Passion cannot be forced on someone. It is there or it is not. Leaders must distinguish between passion and self-conceit. Passion begins as a deep

emotion for a task or objective, whether business or personal. When you are passionate about something, the belief within yourself is infectious to those around you. It becomes a motivator. Self-conceit begins with passion for oneself. It is self-destructing.

I was once very passionate about the job and what I had to offer. I gave it my all.

I was and continue to be passionate about caring for those within my circle of influence.

> Manager to author: *"Sitting behind this desk, I can feel your intensity. You're not going to jump over the desk, are you?"*
> Author: *"Of course not."*

> Author to CEO: *"I will point things out that others would not dare, but I will do so with an eye toward collaborative improvement, growth, and resolve. On the other hand, I do not have much time for those who sugarcoat, card stack, or politicize what otherwise are very obvious conditions."*
> (Note: This communication to the CEO took place after management lambasted the author's presentation and attempts at censure were initiated.)

> CEO to author: *"There is no place in this company for actions against an employee for expressing an opinion."*
> (Our new CEO was well intentioned, but little did he realize. Management did back off however.)

Lead by Example

49) Lead by example. There is no arguing that once a certain management level is reached in an organization, some perks may be deserved, but a value cannot be placed on the leader who sets the example. I have witnessed managers take full advantage of their position with little regard for the employee. Make no mistake, employees never forget it.

Leaders must carry themselves with bearing and confidence. You project what you are and what you think. Carry yourself with pride. A great example is the Marine Corps drill instructor. He is the epitome of bearing. The way he wears his uniform, the way he talks, and his physical presence all command respect.

Especially during tough times, managers must lead by example. I do not consider myself a leader. I just try to lead by example. For instance, twice in the last ten years, I have approached executive management and requested that my merit increase be passed along to other individuals because they were either not receiving a raise or simply being shortchanged. Twice policy has forbidden it. Why? Because there is a limit on what employees can make. Again, to a certain extent, I understand this policy (except when I hear about the millions of dollars given away in bonuses and perks); however, the best employees must be compensated regardless. It is the right thing to do.

Employees will not stay consistently engaged and remain consistently effective unless they see salary adjustments. Without any kind of system of rewards or incentive, the annual increase is all some employees have to look forward to. As mentioned before, this also helps to prevent the "perceptual redress."

Author: *"If he is not getting a raise, and I cannot pass on my merit increase, can I at least get him a bonus or something?"*
Manager: *"It's against policy."*
Author: *"The policy is wrong. This is wrong."*

Decisiveness

50) Leaders are decisive. There is no room for procrastination, regardless of your position. Indecisiveness creates doubt and confusion. Decide! I have witnessed the combination of procrastination and silence rip departments apart. Procrastination rides life, and if you let it, life will pass you by.

In many cases, procrastination is a disease of convenience or laziness, can't get into work on time, can't start that project, but you can get up at 6:00 in the morning—on a Saturday—to participate in that race, competition or hobby. Witness the hoards of shoppers standing in line at 5:00 in the morning on the day after Thanksgiving. Procrastination may be part of human nature, but this nature can be controlled.

When racing the corporate obstacle course, there is no room for procrastination or error. It is easy to get hurt, and there are people in line just waiting to run over you.

"We might as well be talking to a politician, the way he avoided the questions."
Author to colleague after meeting with management

94

on corporate changes

Decisions made in a vacuum inevitably have consequences that cross operational boundaries. Employees must ensure all decisions further organizational strategies and objectives, not just departmental or individual agendas. I have seen a decision made by one group alienate another, and it is usually the result of management not fully understanding the business, not realizing the partiality of the information being provided, or worse, someone pursuing the infamous hidden agenda.

Author: *"You should let them know what we are doing."*
Manager: *"Why?"*
Author: *"No one likes to be blindsided. Informing them is the right thing to do."*
Manager: *"Fine. Put it together."*

Humor

51) A confident leader will possess a good sense of humor. Humor is the medicine for a strict and uptight working environment. Humor alleviates tension.

Manager: *"You're late."*
Employee: *"My car wouldn't start."*
Manager: *"Why wouldn't your car start?"*
Employee: *"I wasn't in it."*
(A coworker shared this incident with me.)

I was attending an executive operations review meeting remotely. Various satellite locations were listening in via conference call and watching the presentation using WebEx, which is a remote conferencing tool. I was bored to tears during one particular session when I noticed a little paintbrush icon at

95

the bottom of the screen. I "innocently" clicked on it, and to my surprise I was able to color the screen. As I spread a rainbow of colors in long sweeping strokes across my computer screen, I did not realize that all the conference attendees were watching me spread an array of colors on the actual presentation. Suddenly the room broke out with laughter, and I was asked to "put away your crayons." Afterwards I contacted the manager in charge of the meeting and apologized. He was actually amused by the whole thing. In reality, no harm was done, and everyone got a good laugh; however, my immediate manager was not so amused, and I heard about it. It was one of those conversations where I just smiled on the inside.

I came across a coaster at a restaurant imprinted with the following quote that stuck with me, *"The ultimate accomplishment is to blur the line between work and play."* Sounds like a challenge.

Technology

52) A leader welcomes advancements in technology. He also recognizes that technology for its own sake is counterproductive- humans make technology work. Information and automation are only tools that must be wielded in a precise and creative fashion; employees are the craftsmen.

Author to information technology executive: *"They have to be nuts if they do not recognize the value of your department. I do, and I appreciate you guys."*

I once paid extra money to purchase a VCR that would allow me to eject the video by using the remote control. I couldn't wait to try it from the comfort of my sofa. The whole thing lost its luster when I realized I still had to get up and take the video out of the VCR. What's the point?

The Marines use technology, but the heart and soul of the Corps is the Marine and his rifle.

Clarity & Endurance

53) Leaders must remain clear-headed and focused. A friend reminded me of that once. A mind clouded with distractions, whether business or personal, cannot process thought efficiently. Employees or management cannot let external circumstances cloud their decision-making or affect their performance. Things happen, and balance cannot always be easy to maintain; however, when at work produce. It is what we get paid for.

Leaders require endurance and must have a clear mind, a strong body, and an awareness of the soul from what I call the "triad of the self." I have sometimes had a weakened leg in this personal triad, and the results manifest themselves in a variety of ways, such as deteriorating relations, physical aches and pains, questionable decision-making, or pure stubbornness. A balanced triad of the self is required for achieving and enduring personal and business success, and it takes effort. A strong triad of the self provides the endurance required to deal with and overcome many of the roadblocks that we encounter through life. A strong triad strengthens the Bull within us.

I can personally attest to the positive physical, emotional, and mental benefits of being in shape and continually working on self-improvement.

In boot camp, The Marine Corps physical fitness test consisted of a timed three-mile run, twenty pull-ups, and I think it was eighty sit-ups in two minutes. I could never master the run, but I never gave up. I was usually one of the last to finish in a very difficult ten-minute mile. I'm not a runner. I hated it and I hated always being in the back. For me, just finishing the run signified personal success. I never gave up. There were times the drill instructor was running right next to me screaming:

"Don't you dare give up!"

If your every day is like that last ten-minute grueling mile, take stock...get clear-headed. Do something about it.

All it takes is:
A decision to do . . .
The commitment to begin . . .
The will to endure . . .

No matter what "it" is, acquire your target, focus, and pull the trigger . . . but don't you dare give up.

A Bull is Born... Welcome to the "Core"

When I first joined the Marine Corps, I had only the slightest idea of what was in store for me. We all–some more than others–grow up in our own little world sheltered by family and friends. At nineteen, I thought I knew it all.

Coming off the bus as Parris Island was my first peek outside of my comfortable little world. As soon as the bus stopped I had some guy in my face, screaming at me, barking orders. It was a rude awakening. Parris Island was where my view of the world and myself would begin to evolve.

During orientation, we sat on the floor and listened to introductions in what seemed to be a very calm and professional atmosphere. I thought, "This isn't so bad." But, when it was over, the speakers turned us over to our drill instructors, and all hell broke lose. These guys were like madmen. The calm of the meeting was shattered by a thunder of screams and people shoving each other, trying to get in line and out of the way of these wide-eyed maniacs. I was shocked beyond words, scared, and felt helpless and lost. I will never forget that first week of boot camp. I

didn't go to the bathroom for a week–and when I was
finally able to go, these guys came in screaming for
everyone to get out. Everything is hurried, and after almost
a week–ouch–I needed some time! Cut it or get your butt
whipped. This was one of the tough lessons in discipline,
not a pretty lesson, but hey, you can't sit there, hold up
your hand, and say, "Wait until I finish." And this was just
the first few days.

It was crazy. One night during the first week, while I stood
at attention, tears welled up in my eyes, and I thought,
"What the hell had I gotten into?" We had one recruit who
tried drinking a bottle of laundry detergent, and I'm not
sure why. We had another recruit who repeatedly bashed
his own head into a concrete pillar. OK. I figured I knew
why he was doing that.

As I stood there wondering how I would make it through
the evening, never mind the rest of the time, our senior drill
instructor issued a challenge to the platoon. He warned
everyone that boot camp was not for the faint of heart, and
he provided one last opportunity for those who wanted to
go home to raise their hands. I don't recall if anyone raised
his hand, I was so consumed with what to do. Then,
suddenly and for a brief moment, our eyes locked, and right
then and there I decided, "I will not quit!" It was almost as
if the challenge was directed right at me. The moment was
defining in that the young romantic ideal of being a Marine
came crashing head on with the reality of what it took to
become one.

Eleven weeks of intense training in the art of discipline and
self-control, I even learned to eat in the Marines. From the
way you talk, to the way you sleep, to the way you walk,

nothing was left to chance.

Prior to embarking on my journey, I was a picky eater. My poor mom never knew what to feed me, especially when I was a preteen. I got better in high school, but was still choosey. But, in Marine Corps boot camp, there are no snacks, no waiters, and no special meals. Eat three squares at your assigned times or go hungry. I ate things I couldn't even describe today. I learned to appreciate food . . . and Mom.

Oh yeah, if you are caught with any snacks in your footlocker, don't bother praying; it will not save you.

Drill instructors are nuts; they are merciless, and I wouldn't have it any other way. But apparently, as crazy as they might act, there are moments of understanding.

Boot camp in winter is . . . well, nasty. I don't particularly like the cold, and the cold reminds me of it once in a while. One particularly chilly day, during marksmanship training, my hands practically froze up. I couldn't shoot. One of my drill instructors came over, took my hand, and rubbed it so that I could finish shooting. Who would have thought?

A little later, the same drill instructor almost broke my fingers because my pinky was sticking out during a rifle drill.

After the usual verbal and physical thrashing, I was ordered into the DI's office. As the drill instructor walked around and sat at his desk, he ordered me to place my hand on the desk and spread my fingers. Needless to say I was a little nervous. He opened the desk drawer and took out a hammer.

When I saw the hammer, my eyes almost popped out and

my balls literally retreated into my stomach. My mind was racing, but I reasoned that pain was only momentary, if you can even call that reasoning. I knew that instinctively I would withdraw my hand as soon as he began to swing, so I leaned forward and placed as much weight on my arm as I could, to ensure that it would not move.

He swung the hammer, and I closed my eyes. I waited. When I peeked, my fingers were still there and the hammer was a couple of inches from my hand. The drill instructor scowled at me and barked, "Get the hell out of my office."

To this day, twenty-three years later, when I drink something, my pinky is nowhere to be seen. Lesson learned.

There actually comes a time when you start to believe you are going to make it. The drill instructors begin to treat you more like a soldier than a maggot. Completing boot camp was a tremendous feeling of achievement.

Those eleven weeks in boot camp changed me. Over the next few years, the core of who I am would continue to develop, but always with a foundation built around what I learned and developed in those eleven weeks . . . discipline, resilience, tenacity, adaptability, loyalty, integrity . . . things that were in me, but just needed to be brought out.

What do the Marines have to do with business? It's simple. In boot camp and in college we learn things that provide a foundation—a Core—for growth and life. How we process and apply what we learn determines how we will live, who we will become. A degree will get you in the door of a company, but that piece of paper does not automatically ingrain in you the traits required to be a strong leader or even a productive employee.

Completing boot camp earns you the right to be called a Marine, but how you apply your Core ultimately determines if you truly are a Marine or just wearing a uniform. My point is this: regardless of the background, a strong Core can allow anyone to succeed in his chosen fields. A strong Core originates in the Triad of the Self. Success is not a given right, it can be self-defined. It is earned . . . it is a behavior . . . it is a thought process, whether in our professional or personal lives. Success does not come from a degree or title. Those things are simply tools and symbols. Success originates in the Core.

The Bull Levels the Field

Everything that happens in a space is a moment in time, and time passes. Time is a precious commodity, never to be relived, reclaimed, or recovered. This awareness and two thoughts allow me to remain level-headed throughout many situations.

First, almost everyone (employees and executives) goes home to a loving family, and their personalities adjust accordingly. I have met many of these families, and I have interacted with most of these individuals at one time or another outside of work. As it turns out, they have souls and feelings–there is a human side. Managers and employees at all levels can display humor, sympathy, love, and affection. There is hope.

The second thing that keeps me level-headed is that undesirable or questionable management styles are restricted to work. Were these individuals to step outside of their organizational safety net and act like they sometimes do at work, these managers would quickly realize that their delegated authority and how they behave does not transition well to the outside world. Depending on the audience or circumstance, it could be a painful experience. This thought amuses me and has allowed me to smile in the midst of some unpleasant encounters.

I use these two thoughts; let's call them "levelers," like individuals who are afraid to speak in public apply the advice to "envision your audience in underwear." The thoughts equalize the playing field.

Decide to Act

Over the years, I have built many relations and friendships throughout the corporate ranks; consequently, my experiences are real and cover a long period of time. Some of the individuals that I have worked with or for have moved on, and few are still with the organization. Some of us have grown and learned from our mistakes, while others refuse to see the light. My hope is that as time passes wounds are healed, friendships are strengthened, and, most importantly, the lessons of the past are applied to a better future.

I know that my circumstances are not unique, and when it comes to the treatment of employees, it seems that my point of view is not very widely embraced. There is no question that companies are in the business of making money, and sometimes tough decisions must be made. But, a combination of the firm leader who leads with empathy and compassion and the employee that performs with integrity and commitment will take the individual and the corporation to new heights.

I believe that the principles I have presented here are

building blocks for success in any endeavor. Remember, life is large, and we are a part of something bigger than us. Sometimes we must reach beyond ourselves.

Finally, I want to share something that is so simple, it almost hurts. It hurts because it is so easy that "I could have . . ."

If every morning you wake up, enter your cage, and step on the wheel for that long run to nowhere, make a decision.

Life is not always easy. Sometimes life throws us a curve, and sometimes there are things that we cannot do anything about, like a debilitating disease. I feel compassion for those whose fate has been cast beyond their control.

But for those of us that can–for those of us who choose–within our reach, within us, is the ability to decide. That is it. Decide. Simple, isn't it? Decide to make these principles a part of your thought process. Decide to do right. Decide to help yourself. Decide to help others. Decide to love. Decide to forgive. Decide to work harder and smarter. Decide to transcend your immediate circumstance and become better and stronger from whatever the experience.

Just Decide. Decide to Act.

Semper Fi

The Self-Fulfilling Prophecy - The Glass House Shattered

The self-fulfilling prophecy is a false prediction or perception that results in a behavior that ultimately makes the original false conception come true.

The facility I worked in toward the end of my career was 1,000 miles away from the corporate headquarters. If you can ever work away from corporate, can be trusted, are self-directed, and still make good money, I highly recommend it, although corporate is the place to be if you plan to move up quickly.

We ("we" represents various departments) had a great set-up. Salespeople loved to bring their customers for tours and demonstrations because the facility always looked good and they knew that the customer would be treated like royalty.

Don't misunderstand. We had our issues just like every other place—inefficiencies and reluctance to change that seem to creep in to any business when complacency sets in.

We had a few areas that required change, and my area was not completely immune. Even here, at my home office, I was sometimes at odds with other managers because of disagreement in management styles.

But we were a family, we got the job done, and we got it done to the satisfaction of most or all of our clients.

Everyone in the facility shared similar views when it came to the business. If someone made a mistake, everyone came together and we did cartwheels, if we had to, and we corrected the error. We understood customer service . . . once. It was just how we operated. We had not "drunk the Kool-Aid." (This expression became the term for apathy toward service and customers after we were purchased.)

A few years ago, the management of the facility and all its operations were turned over to the majority owners of the business. Initially for my department it was a welcomed change, but everyone did not welcome the change, and things began to deteriorate.

The new managers from the new corporate headquarters came into our facility and in no uncertain terms let everyone know what a messed-up operation we had. We were told that we were broken, spoiled, and overpaid and things would have to change. They even accused us of stealing.

They took over an operation and made the mistake of hasty generalizations and assumptions.

These managers went back to their corporate home office and spread their stories based on their unique and biased perceptions. If you believed these guys, we should have been shut down on the spot. It was a presentation based on generalizations, truth, half-truths, and embellishments.

I personally knew the manager they targeted as a thief. I told the new corporate managers there was no way this person, my colleague, would steal from the company. He had faults, but he was no thief. Besides, in my position, I had a firsthand view of operating activities. We had cameras, and I was often in the building on Saturdays or Sundays. No one knew when I was capable of showing up. In spite of my efforts, the new managers did not trust anyone who was not part of their original organization.

Because I was the least of all perceived evil, I was able to establish guarded relations and guarded trust. I was informed that a private investigator had been hired to watch the facility and follow the manager in question. The P.I. never found evidence of wrongdoing, but that didn't seem to matter.

I was told to make sure the facility was locked down.

I was told to review entrance and exit activity.

I was told no one could be trusted.

When I questioned some of the comments or actions, I was told by a manager, "We don't want to give a reason for honest people to become dishonest."

On another occasion a different manager said to me, "Anyone has the ability to steal, given the opportunity."

I never quite understood what I could only call an extremely high level of paranoia. In the corporate world, a manager's paranoia will become a department's albatross.

Projection: the attribution of one's own ideas, feeling, or attitudes to other people or to objects; the externalization of blame, guilt, or responsibility as a defense against anxiety. (*Webster's Ninth New Collegiate Dictionary*)

For one year we trudged along in the facility. We turned into an operation that just wanted to fly under the radar. We just tried to survive. It was a no-win situation, and we knew it. Nothing we did was right.

Change is good, but the managers from the new corporate facility also had not read the principles presented in this book. Change that destroys the morale of employees is not good. These people obliterated the morale of an entire division.

I visited the new corporate headquarters on a number of occasions, and the mood there was always bleak and somber. My visits couldn't be short enough. During one stay, one of their managers I had just met pulled me aside.

Colleague to author: "*Can I be frank with you?*"
Author: "*Shoot.*"
Colleague: "*I've heard about you. Please, just do as you are told, no matter what it is. Otherwise, these guys*

111

will chew you up and spit you out."
Author: *"Yeah, I can see it. I appreciate the heads-up."*

As a result of an acquisition, we were informed that the corporate office had decided to close the facility I worked out of. First we had been stigmatized. Then we would be rendered obsolete. They were looking for an excuse to shut us down, and the excuse just landed in their lap. It was an unfortunate business decision, but I understood the requirement within context of the business reason for the closing.

Because I understood the economic need of our closing, I was resigned to produce and deliver results until the end. I was still getting paid to do a job; however, my job suddenly became one of not finding motivation for employees, but of providing some semblance of hope at the sudden prospect of unemployment for some solid employees. It was a very difficult time.

As a result of the decision to shut down the plant, we were also informed that we would have to train our replacements. If that wasn't a punch in the gut, I don't know what could be, but again, I understood the need to bring other employees up to our level of expertise. Not everyone handled the additional news well.

It is at times like these that a strong Core is needed most.

Among the employees who showed up for training were two of the top operations people (so I was told) from corporate. They were one of the corporate manager's right-hand men. They spent two weeks in my facility training.

When their training was completed and after their

departure, I was informed that we were missing a very expensive and customized tool. It was a tool that only a skilled employee would know how to use; however, because of all the plant closing related activities, I came to the conclusion that anything could have happened. The tool could have been misplaced, lost, or possibly taken by accident when things were being packed.

The incident would be prophetic.

A few days later, rumors began to spread that one of our expensive products that was sold out of the corporate facility had been spotted on an on-line auction. This probably happens often in many companies, but in this case the product in question was a serialized item, and that meant it could be traced.

It is my understanding that a quick investigation ensued, and after a flurry of activity, the "team leaders" (my wording) who had visited my facility for training were fired. Rumor has it these guys were not only pilfering inventory and selling it through on-line auctions, but they also had a business—an actual business—selling stolen products.

I don't like rumors, and there are multiple facets to every story, but the source in this case was reliable and knew the inner workings. He was connected. I verified the firing of these two individuals, which in my mind provided credence to the story in light of all the activity that was taking place at the corporate headquarters during this period of time.

It was an incredible turn of events.

The new corporate managers had done everything possible

to ensure that the higher ups in the company believed the particular location where I resided was a failure. And, as it turned out, in the corporate office, one floor down from where these managers and executives worked eight hours a day, five days a week, the very thing—and everything—they had accused us of was happening right under their very noses.

The problem that I had with this situation was not only the theft–things like this happen in many companies. It was the information that the accused had a side business based on stolen inventory from the self-professed prototypical corporate headquarters. A business!

Over the previous year I had been preached to, incessantly, on right and wrong operations. If I were to go solely by the expectations that had been established for us, then this meant that:
-- Management oversight was lacking in the corporate facility
-- Processes and procedures were broken in the corporate facility
-- Audits were faulty in the corporate facility
-- Security was nonexistent in the corporate facility
-- No loyalty existed in the corporate facility

Supposedly, this was an operation with certified processes... think ISO and Six Sigma.

When a coworker found out this information, he exclaimed, "Holy Six Sigma!" It was a very funny moment.

The process breakdown was happening right under the managers' very noses. What's that saying? "Don't throw stones when you live in a glass house." While they threw rocks, their foundation was crumbling right beneath them.

The corporate managers were living an illusion founded on meaningless metrics and policies. Their numbers said what they wanted, and their policies provided the whipping stick to achieve those numbers.

But the corporate office lost sight of their most important asset.

People.

"It is a sad state of affairs here."
(Colleague to author upon resignation from corporate headquarters)

Appendix A - Get Motivated

Motivation/Self Improvement

Introduce a corporate "values statement" and motivate the troops?
Introduce a corporate "mission statement" and motivate the troops?
Introduce a motivational seminar and motivate the troops?
Introduce a "team-bonding event" and motivate the troops?

NOT!

It simply doesn't work that way.

Here is what works. Practice the principles in this book:
   A. Hire good employees to begin with; correct the mistakes swiftly
   B. Pay well
   C. Treat employees as adults and with dignity
   D. Encourage entrepreneurial behavior
   E. Demand honesty and fairness AT ALL LEVELS
   F. Trust

G. Grow your employees

H. Then do all the fluffy stuff

You can't buy motivation with phony acts of encouragement and meaningless rhetoric.

Behavioral and motivational theories abound. I am no Jung or Maslow, but I can speak from my experiences.

It has been said, "Satisfied needs do not motivate." That may be true, but there are people out there who are never satisfied, so they are always motivated. From a business standpoint, those who are not easily satisfied are typically entrepreneurs or very successful business people. Why? Because there is something inside them that drives and pushes them to a never-ending "next level." Their achievements are drivers in and of themselves. These individuals are constantly raising their own personal bar, and as a result, the bars of those within their circle of influence.

For entrepreneurs in spirit, self-motivation is not a problem. Whether they're working for someone else or self-employed, these are success-oriented individuals. Complacency is not in their vocabulary. The entrepreneurial spirit is a producer, self motivated, a self-starter, and needs minimal or no supervision. Entrepreneurs in spirit are go-to people. Whether in a formal corporate hierarchy or self-employed, these individuals have an independent nature.

For the purpose of discussion, let's say that there are two types of motivational needs, the entrepreneurial spirit and the non-entrepreneurial spirit (ES and NES). Of course, there are varying degrees of motivation inherent within the ES and NES personality depending on the individuals and how they have learned, managed their environment, adapted through the varying stages of growth, and dealt with emotional and physical challenges.

For those who are not entrepreneurially oriented, NES, internal and external motivation is or can be a growing flame in a fireplace that must be continually stoked. The non-entrepreneurial spirit is a work in process. These people require external motivators to keep them really productive.

There is the possibility of an NES individual becoming an ES individual, and this is where I want to focus. A hard- working individual who is not well rounded or polished can begin to recognize that "there is more." This recognition is like a simmering flame. If, for example, she works for a corporation that offers tuition reimbursement, she might decide to attend school at night and further her education. On the other hand, if she does not like school, she might begin reading books to enhance her particular skills or develop new ones. Once she begins to apply her newfound knowledge, she begins to get noticed. Once she begins to get noticed, she can develop the confidence to market herself more effectively. In the corporate world, self-marketing is necessary for success. We all do it to some extent, but some do it better than others.

The recognition that there is more to life than what she has been accustomed to is the spark that ignites her desire to learn more and improve her personal situation as a by-product of becoming more valuable to the organization where she works.

There are many college graduates who are NES personalities. They have a shorter distance to travel to become an ES, but it takes drive and desire. The reason is that they have a foundation for broader thinking. What they build on that foundation will determine their career rate of progression. The developed or well-read individual is better able to recognize opportunity and think critically, and this ability leads to self-improvement.

Self-improvement and continued learning is a must if we are to have any real security in our personal lives. In the twenty-first century, change is urgent. You can be as educated as you want, but the bottom line is the rapid pace of change can easily make an education, except for the fundamentals, obsolete. The reason I believe this is that technological advancements create the need for new skills or knowledge. The only way to keep up with all the change in an information-based world is to continually grow your own knowledge base. The problem is that since "satisfied needs do not motivate," we become complacent. We develop habits and routines that consume our time without actually adding value.

Let's say that on average, we watch two hours of television per night (for me in the old days). Over ten years, that is about 7,300 hours of mind numbing "non-activity." That is a lot of time WASTED. It's part of our routine. Work, hang out with the family, run errands, and maybe hit the gym or something. Many of us are creatures of habit and easily become "routinized," then one day our routine is upset because we learn that our jobs are being shipped overseas, we are being downsized, or our function is no longer required because of some kind of innovation. We are not prepared, and life takes on a new dimension.

Our reaction is typically anger or a feeling of betrayal. In some cases it might even be relief (as was the case for me). We become lost. But it doesn't have to be that way. If you recall my introduction, business is the business of making money. No one owes us anything, but we owe it to our loved ones and ourselves to be vigilant of our lifestyles and earnings potential.

The ES individual will easily adapt to his changing environment. The NES individual, depending on where he sits on the NES scale (approaching ES or not even close), will have a difficult time.

Recently, I read a book titled *Seven Years to Seven Figures*. It is an eye-opening account, with real-life examples, of the need and potential for people to grow their independence and join the ranks of the ES, be it working for someone else or as an independent. Its author, Michael Masterson, also introduces the term "chicken entrepreneur." It is a person who begins to explore other revenue-generating opportunities while remaining in the so-called safety net of a full-time job with benefits. The creation of an alternate source of income has the potential to evolve into a successful business or a source of recurring income to supplement employment income.

According to Masterson, it takes about 1,000 hours to effectively learn a new skill. It takes about 5,000 hours to master it. We can apply this fact in the corporate world or our personal situation. Where can we find time to start reading or learning a new skill?

First, we have to make a decision. We have to decide to act. We have to embrace the reality of our economic climate, personally and professionally. We have to recognize that no one is going to take care of us except ourselves.

Then we must find the time. One thousand hours in the grand scheme of things is nothing, and if used wisely could mean everything. Here are some examples of how I found time to read and work on other skills.

1) Get up earlier–one hour
2) Cut down on happy hours and use the time more effectively–minimum of two hours each incident
3) Leverage the weekends–easy sixteen hours or more, if really intent
4) Maximize my workouts–five hours
5) Skip going out for lunch and eat at my desk– forty-five minutes

From experience, here are some attitude adjustments that are needed by the average NES, including me.
-- I deserve to sleep in.
  Get over it. You'll have plenty of time to sleep when you are dead. Take naps if you have to.
-- I don't like to read.
  Get over it. I don't necessarily get great pleasure from reading all the time, but in my case, the need to do something productive outweighs mental lethargy.
-- I can't find time.
  Yes you can. There are twenty-four hours in a day. Learn to prioritize. For the seriously busy parent, I empathize; however, we can all find one hour in a day to accomplish something worthwhile. But can you find the energy?
-- I don't have the energy.

Then get in shape. Take a vitamin. Eat healthier. But
do something.
-- I don't have the need.
We all have the need. We just don't recognize it until
it's too late.

The message is clear. We need to decide to act and take
control of our destiny by being proactive in our lifestyles.

I started out twenty years ago as a non-entrepreneurial
spirit. I quickly progressed through to an entrepreneurial
spirit and remained in that mode for a few years, but after a
while I did little if any self-improvement. I just didn't see
the need.

Then change happened. The reader of my manifesto can
easily understand why I reverted back to NES. I was no
longer motivated. I had been deconstructed. I had stopped
feeding my mind, and my spirit was in survival mode. Then
one day I picked up a book, and I felt a rumbling inside of
me. That book was the *Seven Habits of Highly Effective
People*. I knew then that I was better than the limitations
being placed on me. I knew then that I was better than my
circumstance and that I was above my immediate
environment. Things began changing for me, or better yet, I
began changing things, and I felt alive again. I started from
within.

In the movie *The Devil's Advocate*, Al Pacino tells Keanu
Reeves, "Never let them see you coming." That is the
approach I adopted. I also recognized that I was a
temporary visitor in a fragile glass house called "the

company," and that the rumbling inside of me needed an opportunity, a chance. The Bull inside of me did not want to play their stupid corporate games (SCG), so my career hibernated while my mind and spirit regained their strength. I kept a low profile–very low. Then opportunity presented itself, and I awoke. I struck, and I was successful in enacting change while a window of opportunity existed. It was change that saved jobs, including mine; at least for the time being.

Appendix B - The Common Sense Approach to Managing Your Dollar

Love is often the desire of something that is difficult to hold unto. Some people just can't hold onto money and may go through extraordinary lengths to acquire it. And even though money does not buy happiness, it certainly buys comfort. But personal comfort has a very personal definition; thus, we must teach our children and ourselves to control money and not let money control us.

The other day I was on the phone with a salesperson who offered me a "great" deal on a product for $3,000.00, a product I did not really need, but was considering. He made a fatal mistake that is apparently standard marketing practice. When he sensed my hesitation, he told me that even though he wasn't making the offer, he wanted to know if I would be more inclined to purchase the item at $2,500.00. The negotiation was over, and he lost the deal.

Why was the negotiation over? Because he knew that I thought the price was high, but he did not change the offer until he sensed that I might not go for it. In my view:

1) He indirectly lied to me
2) My perceived value of the product was destroyed
3) The most important reason; however, *I really DIDN'T NEED IT*

The simple commonsense answer to gaining control of our dollar has nothing to do with the dollar; it has everything to do with our DEFINITION OF NEED.

Last year I decided that I wanted a high-definition flat-screen TV. They are expensive. I want one REAL BAD. I've read about them; I've studied them; and *often*, I visit them at the store. I have two thoughts on this burning need, one stronger than the other:

    a) I deserve it (emotion).
    b) Can I pay cash for it (discipline)?

I have developed financial self-control and a desire to be debt-free.

True financial control comes from having the ability to do two things. First, you must buy only what you need or can afford without going into debt. The only exceptions to the debt rule are a car and a home. A car provides you with the means to get around efficiently and earn a living. IT IS NOT A STATUS SYMBOL. A home appreciates in value over time. A HOME IS DEBT UNTIL YOU SELL IT.

I knew a person who was in debt. He was a good man and an avid motorcyclist. There came a point when he decided to declare bankruptcy. I suggested he sell the motorcycle to help pay off his debt. His response was, "I'd rather lose an arm." It was an emotional attachment to a material thing that came at a high price, and he was willing to pay it. He made a decision.

Second, you must control and balance lifestyle with increasing income. The more money you make should not mean the more money you spend, UNLESS you have accumulated savings and investments that permit spending without incurring debt. There is one caveat. You must have a means of recurring (or passive) income that permits you to spend without depleting your savings. There are some possible ways of doing this (three recommended by experts):

1) Investing in the stock market
   a. If you have a 401(k) offering at work, don't even think of not participating
2) Investing in real estate
3) Investing in a business
4) Steady employment (in today's economic climate, no job is ensured)
5) Win the lottery (it's possible, but don't hold your breath)
6) Have a rich relative who really, really likes you (check your family tree)
7) Hit it big at the casinos (will cost a lot more than the lottery and is unlikely to happen)

The YOUNGER YOU START to save and invest, THE MORE SUCCESS YOU WILL ACHIEVE by leveraging time and compound interest; however, no matter how old you are, if you haven't started, you must act now and begin to save.

I was reading the other day that the United States has a

negative savings rate. No one, it seems, is saving money. On top of that, with housing prices out of control, many people have leveraged themselves into no-win situations by borrowing excessively. For those people, an unforeseen reduction in salary or a small bump in interest rates could spell financial disaster.

Saving money is not as difficult as it seems if we put aside the need for immediate gratification or the thought that we deserve something. The first and probably most important step is to take out a percentage of your paycheck and save it. Before you spend one cent from your salary, you must take some amount and sock it away. Put it in the bank or invest it. The higher the percentage that you take out and save, the faster you will build your portfolio of security. The younger you start, the better, but always "pay yourself first."

If we add up the money that we spend over a period of time on things we REALLY DON'T NEED, we will find it easy to make some minor adjustment in our lifestyles that will provide us with the means to save. If you are not sure you can do this, here are a couple of personal examples.

I was eating lunch out about four times a week at $7 bucks a pop. Over the course of a year, that cost adds up to about $1,400.00. Do I really need to eat out that bad . . . four times a week? I think not. I now bring a bag lunch to work more often than not and sock away what I am not wasting.

I was buying an eighteen-ounce coffee every morning on the way to work at about $1.25 a pop–about $300.00 per year. Makes no sense to me. They serve coffee at work.

If you make some minor lifestyle adjustments and put money away before you spend it on anything else, you are effectively reducing the amount of money you waste and are making an investment in your secure future.

Surprises abound in life, and one of the worse surprises of all is the sudden lack of money because of a lack of a savings plan. I have felt this pain within my family, and it is something we should all work very hard to avoid. Many of us don't think about things like retirement or an emergency fund until the need for one has become a reality, and by then . . . IT IS TOO LATE!

If you make only enough money to shelter and feed yourself, then a part-time job or side business must be a strong consideration, if only until a financial buffer of some sort is built.

The sacrifice we think we are making today in order to save for an unknown future is nothing compared to the pain of a sudden job loss, a death of a key provider without insurance, or retirement without savings for a comfortable living when we need it most.

I want many things out of life, but the desire for immediate feel-good activities or status-building symbols is tempered by the fact that when I borrow money, I HAVE TO PAY IT BACK.

Eight years ago, when my Honda Civic began acting up after about 100,000 miles, I wanted a BMW. For some reason, I really like that car. They are not cheap, but at the time, I could afford one. Instead, I bought the most basic Honda Civic, my fourth.

It was so basic that when my boss sat in it he pointed to the window lever and jokingly asked me, "What's that?" Of course, he had electric windows in his car.

The reason I provide the Civic example is that it again points out the difference between an emotional decision and a disciplined decision based on the NEED for transportation, not how I look or feel while being transported. I paid the car off early and kept taking what would be the payment and putting it in the bank.

I'm not saying spending money on a luxury item is wrong. I'm saying if it puts you in debt with no return on your investment, it is unnecessary.

We can have fun and experience things as we grow older, but always with an eye toward our financial future.

Learn, Invest and Save.

Below I recommend four very good books. The authors of these books provide sound and experienced advice on how to gain control of your financial life. Keep in mind that there are many authors with many ideas. You have to filter out what is right for you and always remember that no one person knows it all. If someone claims to, don't trust him or her.

Secrets of a Millionaire Mind - by T. Harv Eker

The Five Lessons a Millionaire Taught Me - by Richard Paul Evans

The Automatic Millionaire - by David Bach

Rich Dad, Poor Dad - by Robert Kiyosaki

The rest is up to you.

Appendix C - Streamlining Project Management

Over a period of eight years, I have spent approximately thirty months in project implementations. Specifically three SAP implementations (one of which involved the consolidation of two operating companies) and one SAP upgrade. SAP stands for Systems, Applications, and Products in data processing.

For those not familiar with the subject, the last time I looked, SAP was the bestselling software for running an organization. From my experience, I can't really argue with that assessment if IT IS DONE RIGHT.

The projects I worked on shared similar characteristics:
- ✓ Lack of buy-in from users
- ✓ Inadequate time
- ✓ Lack of executive support or understanding of operating needs
- ✓ The massive overworking of employees starting at the midpoint of the project
- ✓ Not enough planning

131

"The definition of insanity is doing the same thing over and over again and expecting a different result." This quote, depending on where you look, is attributed to Albert Einstein or Benjamin Franklin. I use it here only in the context of project methodology.

Is there a better way? I suspect there is. A company decides to do a project and brings in consultants. The consultants arrive with their experiences and preconceived notions of what tools, forms, or processes need to be used. The company reasons that they are paying for the consultants; therefore, the consultants know best. And, of course, the projects take a long time, but there seems to never be enough time. It's quite a conundrum.

A project manager or team leader must have the capacity to say something is not needed or something would take too long and could be completed in a different way unique to the organization.

A consultant must be flexible and open-minded to change, even within her area of expertise.

There are many facets to a project plan (people, budgets, processes, time) and every organization is different. Below are some of the events or actions that must take place, *at a minimum*, for any project to be fully realized.

The first thing any corporation must do before embarking on a major project is prepare the employees for change. Some people have been doing the same job, the same way, for a long time. Their initial reaction to major change is something like resentment, and some employees will even consciously or unconsciously attempt to sabotage some of the initiatives. But, as The Borg, of Star Trek fame, have stated, "Resistance is futile."

Contrary to popular thought, embracing change is the only means of job security. Yes, things will be different and some individuals may be relocated or some jobs may be eliminated. Unfortunately, "collateral damage" is inevitable, but in a well-run company, minimized.

You can prepare employees for change by communicating the reasons and the advantages of the proposed changes and then keeping them informed of project progress. A once-a-month newsletter works fine, or some other form of communication after any significant milestone is reached.

Important Point:
No surprises and eliminate the fluff.

A PowerPoint presentation on the subject of change presented by department managers helps employees understand how the business world is a dynamic environment and change is the only way corporations survive and prosper in a competitive landscape.

There are also books on change and dealing with change that can be made available to employees. The trick here would be getting some employees to actually read them and then to read them with an open mind. This is the least preferable method for me.

I believe accepting change, and the job insecurity it often brings, is one of the biggest obstacles any major project initiative is faced with. But, as with all obstacles, reluctance to change can be overcome.

One often overlooked, but effective method of achieving buy-in is to simply get the user community involved in some of the decision-making.

Having addressed the change acceptance issue, here is my short list of the absolute "must haves" to ensure the successful completion of a project.

1) **The highest-level executives must very visibly and emphatically provide their approvals and endorsements** not only for the project, but also for the teams on the project. The project members should be extensions of these leaders.

2) **Only place your best employees on a project.** If your best employee is too valuable to dedicate his time to the company's success, then you have not done your job in cross training and building your bench strength.

3) **Project team members must be trusted and empowered decision-makers.** If you must get more than one level of approvals from executives who have no clue of process details, then you are wasting time and the right people are not on the project. The only time an executive should have to get involved is to mediate a dispute or approve a recommended corporate-level change.

4) **Eliminate bureaucracy and leverage commonsense.** A perfect example of this

requirement was how the information technology group used accounting rules to determine if a system change was warranted. Here is how the process worked: If I wanted I.T. to perform a function, I had to submit a form with signatures on it. The I.T. department would then estimate the time required to complete the task and multiply it by an hourly rate to arrive at the cost of the labor involved. So far so good. The problem was that the department used some obscure cost-accounting-loaded labor rate of around $90.00 per hour. Who the hell makes $90.00 per hour?! I argued that any loaded labor rate should apply only after labor capacity had been reached. In other words, during the course of a standard workday, the IT department had to be in the facility and complete work. Only after they had too much work and an outsourcing or overtime requirement arose should any type of cost be weighed.

Project priorities should be based on the financial return to the organization or the improvement to a process that may not always be measurable in dollars, but may be measurable in the speed or efficiency with which a particular function could be completed.

When drafting a justification for change takes longer than the actual work on the system to complete the change, something is wrong.

5) **Rationalize your business processes.** Do not assume you have the best business practice. Review and discuss the operations. If possible research what

other companies are doing. This is the time to make things better, not remain at status quo or live in the past.

I have seen countless acts of unintentional sabotage of the potential for improvements by simply taking a bad process and transferring it to a new system.

6) **Ensure that all team members are adequately trained.** During one project I was actually creating training documentation before I received any training. The decision-makers, pressed for time, were devoid of reasoning.

The effectiveness of training can make or break an operation after go-live. **Invest heavily in training.**

7) **The team leaders must supervise workshops.** A workshop should result in something–some conclusion or decision–and these results should be documented.

8) **Ensure that all meetings and communications are grounded with substance and relevance.** I repeat, **substance and relevance.**

9) **Provide ample time to complete a project.** When a company is going through change, things might come up that were not foreseen. A project must have some flexibility to account for these occurrences.

One year, while taking the time to learn more about the system we were implementing, I came across a function that we were not told about and would greatly benefit us. When I approached the consultant, he tried to blow it off because it was "not in scope." Well, that did not go over well, and I got what we needed. The lesson here is the need for flexibility and reinforcement of empowered team leaders.

During another project many operational improvements were negated or avoided by sticking with the status quo. During the consolidation of two operating companies, one of them assumed they had the best practices. There was no discussion. There might have been good reasons for this, but I don't know them.

Do what is right for the business in the long term, not just immediate or short-term questionable results.

10) **Replace or remove unproductive or uncooperative employees from project involvement.** As obvious as that sounds, often these individuals get lost until a major mistake occurs.

11) **Project teams must ensure their decisions do not adversely affect other teams downstream.** This will typically come out either in a meeting or during initial testing.

We often worked in a "war room" where all the teams worked in the same physical location. On a few occasions I got involved in conversations that would change a course of action simply because someone had not fully understood the implications to other areas of a particular decision.

12) **Consultants need to be managed.** They play a critical role in any project success, but they are only human and bring natural biases to the table based on their past experiences. I have learned much from some consultants and have remained friends with a couple of these individuals.

Companies have many inefficient processes. How do I know? It's how quality initiatives like Six Sigma and ISO catch on. Identifying the underlying cause of inefficiencies is one area where consultants can play a strong role. They do not come into the organization as part of a clique or with any friends or processes to protect. The contractor can look at a function with an objective eye.

During my last project, we had very knowledgeable consultants, but a few involved were just not needed. Here are three specific examples:

One person's role, every morning, was to review the previous day's activities in a meeting. He then spent the rest of his time going around asking everyone if they were meeting deadlines. We used to joke that one of our kids could be making some money doing the same thing. Frankly, it was a waste of a valuable resource.

We also had a couple of individuals helping us create training manuals. They provided the template for us to use, the team members did all the work, and then training consultants evaluated the result. Again, this job was something that did not need to be outsourced. The consultants obviously could not comment on the value of the content because they did not understand the business, but we created pretty manuals.

Finally, we had a "change management" team. It put out surveys and letters and had meetings and conference calls wherein people had a chance to voice their opinions and concerns, and, as one colleague put it, "for what?" Enough said.

I talked to many people who attended these gatherings, and substance and relevance were the missing ingredients.

In the project world of very tight timelines, incentive-driven deadlines, and document and process paralysis, FLEXIBILITY AND COMMONSENSE ARE PRICELESS.

13) **Permit liberal security during the implementation.** This setup provides project teams and users the flexibility to explore the system and discover tools that could improve an operation even beyond what they may have been taught or provide information that may not be readily available.

After going live, do not limit security in such a way that it takes multiple people to complete one task, when, with the proper process, one person would suffice. **Rewrite job descriptions, if you must.**

The I.T. department must have the resources and

ability to implement ongoing process improvements based on user training and recommendations. I.T. can be a valuable ally and resource for the company or they can be a hindrance. Executives should ensure that I.T. is staffed appropriately and understand their role as a customer service entity to the user community.

In my current environment, the organization continues to shortchange itself. The capabilities of SAP are massive, yet we seem to be tapping into only ten percent. Why? Because it seems management does not find value in further development. Why? Because no one is sent for further formal training to leverage the strengths and capabilities of this system. Why? It's too expensive and there are not enough resources.

The project turns into an investment that becomes stagnant, and without continued training and growth, bad habits creep back into the processes. Maybe this situation will change someday.

14) **Stop blaming the system for your operating problems** if you do not plan, change, train, configure, test, and execute properly.

I understand that the planning of a project is a massive undertaking and certain things will fall through the cracks. But as I mentioned before, beware of the escalating commitment. **Recognize what may not be working and move swiftly to correct it.**

Even as I write this list of project must do's, I must remind myself that there is a lot more to a project than this;

however, I have seen the consequences of not taking these particular action items seriously enough.

The most important part of a project and the measure of its success should not be turning on the switch and solely if it is within budget or on time. The true measure of a project's success must be how much it improved efficiency and reduced costs.

- ✓ If employees must complete more transactions to complete a simple process, it is not success.
- ✓ If employees must resort to spreadsheets and databases to manage their processes, it is not success.
- ✓ If employees must resort to spreadsheets and databases to report on their processes, it is not success.
- ✓ If employees must resort to manual mass processing of information that can be automated, it is not success.
- ✓ If standard reporting tools are not activated or generally made available, it is not success.
- ✓ If interfaces between systems do not match, it is not success.
- ✓ If automated processes do not allow for flexibility in data processing, it is not success.
- ✓ If information cannot be found, it is not success.
- ✓ If the collection of revenue is compromised in any way, it is not success.
- ✓ If a customer cannot easily and readily interface with the company, it is failure.

Look, I don't expect large-scale projects to go off without some problems or setbacks. It is how these problems are handled that can mean the difference between success and anything less than success in varying degrees.

In short, as a company, get your act together before you even think of investing in external improvements. I think that an organization invests a lot of time and money with the hope that a new system will fix all its woes. This couldn't be further from the truth. A company must embrace and enact change prior to the start of any project.

Appendix D - More "What Were They Thinking" Moments and How to Avoid Them

This is a good follow-up to Appendix C on project management. There are many kinds of projects–small projects, big projects, expensive projects, and projects that make you wonder, "What were they thinking?"

The division where I spent the better half of my career was a high-end, high-value business. The equipment was large and expensive, and the inventory, like the equipment, was large and expensive. As a result of a couple of corporate acquisitions, the value of the business we offered our customers was diluted. Every attempt was made at commoditizing how we managed our processes and dealt with our customers.

Inventory is inventory. Service is service. All customers are the same, right?

Wrong!

Project A was the consolidation of a service parts warehouse from two locations for two different business models into one location serving both business models. One type of inventory tended to be bulky and expensive. The other type of inventory was smaller and cheaper.

For the more expensive inventory we had an inspection process for field returns coming back to the distribution center. Whenever certain types of product were returned to the main warehouse they went through two levels of inspection. One was at the receiving dock, and one was a more technical inspection performed by a technical department.

As a result of the inspections, we found that seventeen percent of parts returned as good were actually bad, either because of obsolescence or some kind of damage. These parts never made it back into saleable inventory, and more importantly, they never made it back to the vendor for credit on goods parts. Saleable inventory was not corrupted as a result of this process. Our vendor was very pleased with how we managed our business.

During the transition from one location to the other, this information was clearly communicated to management, and the response:

"We don't have the resources, and it would be too expensive to put something in place."

Fast forward a year or so.

144

Because of a process where our primary vendor regularly requested "good" inventory returns for credit and the lack of any inspection process on our part, the company was hit with a significant bill (The number I heard was about $100K) for returning good product back to the vendor that ended up being damaged, used, or obsolete.

I don't know the exact dollar value of the invoice, but the vendor had to come in and conduct audits. The last I heard, management was looking to get some kind of inspection process in place. I guess people do listen, when it hits them in the pocket. Go figure.

Project B was a bigger "what were they thinking" moment. As a result of a corporate purchase, a third major distribution center was acquired. We didn't need three distribution centers, so a decision was made to close down one of them and consolidate all service parts inventory into the new one.

The corporate managers gave the project a name and had a project team assigned. That's how *important* the project was. Although I was not involved, I get a chuckle when I picture the meetings and conference calls where Gantt charts and PowerPoint slides were used to show "progress."

I wasn't there, but it is what management does–lots of meetings, lots of talking, lots of fluff and little substance.

As I stated earlier in my manifesto, I don't know what goes on in the executive offices and why some decisions are made, but, once again, I can only shake my head on this one.

The interesting thing about this particular project is that even though it affected the facility where I worked, no one really took an interest in how we ran our part of the business. No one called and spoke with us. No one asked us any questions except for some basic data requests regarding volumes and dimensions; other than that, nothing.

Well, they pulled the trigger on the project and in a nutshell, business stopped functioning. Simply stated, parts stopped shipping, and customers were screaming bloody murder.

I can't imagine what this screw-up was costing the company. But wait . . . it gets better.

I was asked to attend a conference call wherein I would be informed of the dire situation.

I was asked if I'd be willing to go away for two weeks and provide the badly needed training and support that was apparently lacking. The reader needs to keep in mind that I was one month away from being released because relocation was not an option for me, at the time.

Of course I agreed to do whatever was necessary to salvage what was left of the project. So off I went to assist those who never needed assistance.

Why did these projects crash?

First, the thing that immediately struck me was an apparent lack of communication and flexibility. In both instances, a lack of communication and an unwillingness to listen and be flexible caused major problems.

When a company, a department, or even individual managers believe they have all the answers and the best processes and "know what is best" without taking the time to learn and understand the nuances associated with an operating company or system, it is a recipe for failure.

Second, there was such a rush to get project B completed before the end of the fiscal year that bad assumptions and questionable compromises were made. How else do you account for such a disastrous conclusion to a project with a team and a fancy name?

What is it that causes a company to rush into and finish a project when failure is all but assured? Is it stock price implication? Budget concerns? Bonus plans at risk? I wish I knew. But again, from my experience, even if I had a crystal ball and could predict the future with certainty, I doubt people in upper management would listen.

Why? Because, they didn't come up with it. It wasn't their crystal ball.

What I do know is what I saw when I arrived at my destination to put in twelve- to fourteen-hour days for two weeks to help fix a mess that was created by someone else. It wasn't pretty.

Where does the vendor-client relationship fall into all this? Does anyone even care what our customers are feeling?

I point out these two instances from many because they are endemic of the attitudes and questionable management tactics used to achieve an end. The one who ultimately pays the price is our client.

If in our zeal to reduce costs we damage the client relationship and hurt employee morale, then obviously something is wrong with the decision-making process.

There is a rug and there is a broom and there is a mess. And the mess underneath the rug just keeps growing because someone just keeps sweeping things under the rug. Eventually (and I doubt it), someone will notice the growing mountain and start asking questions, but a question asked does not imply a solution to a problem. The root or source of the problem must be uncovered.

A speaker at a conference I attended stated, "Money loves speed." I agree. But, reckless speed kills.

From the looks of things, client relationships and employee morale are just not that important. I know that isn't completely true. I'm just searching for answers, and I believe they lie in the heart of this manifesto.